UML Database Modeling Workbook

Michael Blaha

Published by:

Technics Publications, LLC
966 Woodmere Drive
Westfield, NJ 07090 U.S.A.
www.technicspub.com

Edited by Carol Lehn
Cover design by Mark Brye

ISBN, print ed.   978-1-9355045-1-1
First Printing 2013
Printed in the United States of America
Library of Congress Control Number: 2013938641

To the memory of my friend, colleague, and mentor Bill Huth.

I first met Bill during my early years of consulting, then at Johnson Controls. Bill was a pivotal influence on my thinking, experiences, and career both from a technical and management perspective. I will miss our stimulating discussions and his friendship.

Preface

When building an application, your job is not to do what the customer says. Your job is to solve the problem that the customer is imperfectly describing. Accordingly, you must pay attention to the hidden true requirements and interpret and abstract what the customer tells you. In addition, you must recognize arbitrary business decisions that could easily change.

This is why data modeling is important. Data modeling can help you set the scope of an application and communicate your understanding to the customer. You can probe their problem description. You can consider different representations, and how they affect development effort, as well as effectiveness. A sound data model naturally leads to a solid database design and good performance.

There is a growing awareness of the power of using the UML (Unified Modeling Language) for understanding and representing databases. The UML is not only helpful for programming, but it is also helpful for databases. This book can teach you how to use the UML for databases. You learn by reading a bit, trying your hand at some exercises, then reading some more, and doing exercises some more. I've created exercises from a variety of problem domains and have tried to give reasonable answers.

This book is novel in that it teaches UML data modeling by comparison to a conventional database notation — Information Engineering (IE). If you are experienced and already know IE, you can leverage your existing knowledge and learn the UML faster. If you don't know IE, you can ignore the IE references and still obtain most of the book's benefits.

Why Is This Book Needed?

Data modeling is a critical skill for both application and enterprise software, but it is difficult to learn. There is a big difference in software results when data models are constructed expertly vs. when they are constructed badly. The UML can help data modelers think more deeply and abstractly; they can communicate better with customers than with a physical database notation. Briefly stated, developers can spend less time and develop better data models.

Many database practitioners are aware of the UML and have interest, but are uncertain about how to proceed. This book explains the UML via a notation (IE) that many data modelers already understand. The exercises can help readers practice and gain confidence. The tests can help readers measure their comprehension.

Who Should Read This Book?

This book has multiple audiences. It is targeted at practitioners but is also suitable for students:

- **Application architects**. Application architects help determine the focus of an application and drive that focus into the resulting software. They have to pin down the requirements, understand the requirements, determine what is in and out of scope, and set key software abstractions. These tasks revolve about models and often data models.

- **Enterprise architects**. Enterprise architects reach beyond a single application and address the needs of an entire enterprise. The suite of applications for an enterprise must provide the required business functionality and work well together. There is no better way to harmonize applications than by modeling them deeply and aligning the models. With models, gaps become apparent and problems can be resolved.

- **Data modelers**. The book can teach basic skills to novice data modelers. Experienced data modelers can pick up the UML notation by leveraging their existing knowledge.

- **Programmers**. Many developers already use the UML for programming. This book shows how to use the UML for databases.

- **Students**. The book is well suited for commercial data modeling courses, as well as university courses, in the areas of software engineering and databases.

What You Will Find

Chapter 1 explains the premise for the book and sets the context. Chapter 2 presents a data modeling example that is used throughout the book (the online retail example).

Part 1 (Chapters 3–5) covers basic data modeling concepts — the minimal concepts that you will need to be able to start constructing UML data models. The chapters explain concepts, provide examples, and compare UML constructs to IE.

Part 2 (Chapters 6-10) explains advanced data modeling concepts. You will need these concepts to construct UML data models for large and complex problems. Chapter 10 addresses model quality (how to prepare sound models and how to measure quality).

Parts 1 and 2 cover UML data modeling in detail. But there are several kinds of models that you can construct. They all involve the same building blocks, but use them in different ways. Part 3 (Chapters 11-14) explains these kinds of models and why they are important.

Part 4 (Chapters 15-16) shows how to take data models and use them for design. Chapter 15 discusses how to create code for the initial empty database structure. Chapter 16 shows how to use the data model as a guide for writing database queries.

The Appendix answers all exercises and test questions in the book.

Comparison with Other Books

Three items distinguish this book from other offerings:

- **Focus on the UML**. This book teaches data modeling in terms of the UML. Few database books use the UML.
- **Teaching the UML by comparison to IE**. I don't know of any books that teach UML data modeling by comparison to a conventional database notation. It is clearly beneficial for readers to leverage their existing knowledge.
- **Emphasis on exercises and tests**. Few books can match the depth of exercises in this book.

There are many database modeling and design books on the market. The following books are especially relevant:

- David C Hay. *UML and Data Modeling: A Reconciliation*. Westfield, New Jersey: Technics Publications, 2012.

    Hay's book is a philosophical exploration about the UML and databases. In contrast, this book focuses on the nuts and bolts of using UML and IE together to build database applications, systems, and enterprises.

- Steve Hoberman. *Data Modeling Made Simple, Second Edition*. Bradley Beach, New Jersey: Technics Publications, 2009.

    Hoberman's book has a clear, crisp explanation of database modeling. He is especially effective at reaching database and data modeling novices. In contrast, this book presumes a higher level of reader skill. Hoberman's book can get practitioners started in database modeling and this book can build on the start.

Some of my past books cover UML and databases but they do not leverage prior understanding of conventional database notations.

About the Author

Since 1994 I have been a consultant and trainer in conceiving, architecting, modeling, designing, and tuning databases. I have worked with dozens of organizations around the world. I have authored seven U.S. patents, six books, and many articles. I received my doctorate from Washington University in St. Louis and am an alumnus of GE Global Research in Schenectady, New York.

If you have questions, comments, and suggestions about this book, please send an email to blaha@computer.org. You can also use this email address to inquire about my teaching and consulting services.

Acknowledgments

I thank my reviewers for their thoughtful advice: Donna Burbank, Steve Hoberman, Roger Kelly, R. Raymond McGirt, and Keith Wanta. I especially thank Raymond McGirt for working the exercises and sharing the details of his answers. Nathan Wilson also had some useful comments.

I used several tools in the writing of this book. Specifically, I used Enterprise Architect to create the UML models and then rekeyed them with the Framemaker desktop publishing software for a precise layout. I used ERwin to create IE models and also typeset them with Framemaker. I tested the SQL code with Microsoft's SQL Server.

I thank Sass Babayan for teaching me more about data warehouses. In the past few years I've had the opportunity to work with Sass on a very large medical data warehouse and it has been informative.

And finally I'd like to thank Steve Hoberman. He not only is the publisher of this book, but also a valued reviewer. Steve contributed database insights, in addition to his advice as a fellow author. I plan on publishing my next book with Steve and encourage other database authors to consider doing likewise.

Good luck with this workbook. I hope you find it interesting, informative, challenging, and worth an investment of your time.

Michael Blaha
Wildwood, Missouri, USA
blaha@computer.org

Contents

Contents

1

Introduction

Welcome to the UML Database Modeling Workbook! This book can teach you database modeling through concise explanation, practice with exercises, and a series of self-assessment tests. The book is targeted at software professionals, such as the following:

- **Application architects**. Their guidance for applications often revolves about models and data models.

- **Enterprise architects**. They reach beyond a single application and address the needs of an enterprise. There is no better way to harmonize applications than by modeling them deeply and aligning the models.

- **Data modelers**. The book can teach basic skills to novice data modelers. Experienced data modelers can pick up a new notation (the UML) by leveraging their existing knowledge.

- **Students**. The book is suited for commercial data modeling courses as well as university courses.

1.1 Data and Databases

Data is a corporate resource. It's the lifeblood of most organizations and critical to their endeavors. Data provides an organization's memory — its customers, competitors, products, orders, employees, equipment, locations, objectives, plans, sales, and expenses.

Data is found in many forms. A simple technique is to store data in files; this can work well for small quantities. A more sophisticated approach is to store data in a database. Database software carefully manages data, offering multi-user access while protecting against accidental loss. Database software can also enforce constraints that boost the quality of data, reducing corruption from data entry mistakes and programming errors. Databases provide flexible data access that reduces development cost while achieving fast performance.

The dominant database paradigm today is the relational database. A relational database presents data in the form of tables. Normally each table has a primary key that uniquely identifies individual records. Tables connect via foreign keys, a reference to a unique identifier, usually the primary key. A major feature of relational databases is referential integrity — developers can declare foreign key references and system software keeps the references valid.

Relational databases are certainly powerful, but they can be difficult to use. The notion of a table seems simple, but a database is anything but simple. Hundreds or thousands of tables interconnect via foreign keys to form a complex graph. This is why data modeling is important. Data modeling lets stakeholders visualize the structure of a database, understand the critical concepts, consider alternate representations, and then summarize the results in a meaningful diagram.

1.2 Models and Data Models

A *model* is a representation of some aspect of a problem that lets you thoroughly understand it. A *data model* is a model that describes how data is stored and accessed, usually for a database. Developers must understand a problem before attempting a solution. Most database models are expressed as graphical diagrams and, by their form, appeal to human intuition. There are many reasons for constructing models:

- **Better quality**. Your application can be no better than the underlying thought. ACM Turing award winner Fred Brooks contends "that conceptual integrity is the most important consideration in system design." [Brooks-1995]

- **Reduced cost**. You can shift your activities towards the relatively inexpensive front end of software development and away from costly debugging and maintenance.

- **Faster time to market**. It takes less time to deal with difficulties at the conceptual stage than to deal with them when software has been cast into code.

- **Better performance**. A sound model simplifies database tuning.

- **Communication**. Models reduce misunderstandings and promote consensus among developers, customers, and other stakeholders.

- **Fewer mistakes**. Rigorous modeling improves the quality of the data. You can weave constraints into the fabric of a model and the resulting database.

The bottom line is that models provide the means for building quality software in a predictable manner.

This book uses the Unified Modeling Language (UML) as its primary notation. In addition, we use Information Engineering (IE) to clarify the meaning of UML constructs and illustrate aspects of database design.

1.3 The Unified Modeling Language (UML)

The *Unified Modeling Language (UML)* [Blaha-2005] [Rumbaugh-2005] [OMG – Object Management Group] is a graphical language for modeling software. The UML has a variety of notations of which one (the class model) concerns databases. The UML *class model* specifies classes (entity types) and their relationship types. The resulting model sets the scope and level of abstraction for subsequent development. There are several benefits of using the UML for database modeling:

- **Communication**. The UML provides a means for communicating with customers. The UML is more concise than traditional database notations and defers database details. Thus the UML suppresses database gore such as primary keys, foreign keys, indexes, and referential integrity that is important for implementation but is not needed for specifying a problem. This helps customers focus on requirements and scope.

- **Abstraction**. The UML lets modelers focus on the essence of a problem — the key concepts and how they relate — and avoid distracting notational clutter. The resulting concise models help developers envision modeling alternatives and explicitly consider their options, such as different data modeling patterns [Blaha-2010].

- **Precision**. The UML class model has several helpful features (most notably association classes and qualifiers) not found in most other database notations.

The UML is popular with programmers, but is used less often by database developers — this is the primary drawback of the UML. One reason is technical — the UML creators loaded the UML with many programming details that are extraneous to databases. Another reason is that few UML tools support database design. The irony is that the programming jargon is superficial, and in reality, the UML has much to offer for database applications.

1.4 Information Engineering (IE)

Information engineering (IE)[*] is a prominent database modeling notation that has been in use for many years. IE was popularized by James Martin and Clive Finkelstein in the 1980s and is oriented towards database design. IE focuses on details such as tables, keys, and indexes. This book uses IE as a secondary notation because it is familiar to many database practitioners. Furthermore, IE's attention to database detail is helpful for explaining nuances of the UML.

IE lacks a standard notation. Rather, there are several variants that express the same underlying concepts. This book uses the ERwin database modeling tool as the arbiter of IE notation.

1.5 Using UML and IE Together

The database literature traditionally distinguishes among three kinds of models:

- *Conceptual model* — focuses on major entity types and relationship types. Provides a high-level overview. Has no attributes.

- *Logical model* — fleshes out the conceptual model with attributes and lesser entity types.

- *Physical model* — converts the logical model into a database design. The emphasis is on physical constructs such as tables, keys, indexes, and constraints.

The UML is effective for conceptual and logical data models. IE is effective for physical data models.[†] The notations complement each other's strengths and are effective to use together.

Our development process uses both notations. We start with the UML to conceive the abstractions of an application and converge with customers on content and scope. Then we translate the ideas into IE and add database details. From IE, we generate database code. The

---

* Please note: In this book, IE is an acronym for Information Engineering (and is not referring to Internet Explorer).

† Strictly speaking, UML and IE are equally good for conceptual modeling. But the UML is usually better for logical modeling, which comes after conceptual modeling.

UML is good for abstract modeling but not for database design. IE is good for database design but not for abstract modeling. Both notations are useful, but each has its place. We maintain both models as revisions occur, and use agile development to build an application as a series of iterations.

1.6 Chapter Summary

A model is an abstraction of a problem that lets you thoroughly understand it. A data model is a model that describes how data is stored and accessed, usually for a database.

This book uses the UML class model as its primary notation, and IE as a secondary notation. The UML is effective for conceptual and logical data models. IE is effective for physical data models. The notations complement each other's strengths and are effective to use together.

Bibliographic Notes

The UML class model is one of a score of approaches descended from the seminal entity-relationship notation of [Chen-1976]. The class model is essentially just another Chen dialect, but one that has the backing of a standard (sponsored by the Object Management Group). [Elmasri-2011] is a good general database reference. Hernandez, Hoberman, and Teorey are good data modeling references. [Burbank-2011] has helpful advice for using the ERwin database modeling tool.

References

[Blaha-2005] Michael Blaha and James Rumbaugh. *Object-Oriented Modeling and Design with UML, Second Edition*. Upper Saddle River, NJ: Prentice Hall, 2005.

[Blaha-2010] Michael Blaha. *Patterns of Data Modeling*. New York: CRC Press, 2010.

[Brooks-1995] Frederick P. Brooks, Jr. *The Mythical Man-Month, Anniversary Edition*. Reading, Massachusetts: Addison-Wesley, 1995.

[Burbank-2011] Donna Burbank and Steve Hoberman. *Data Modeling Made Simple with CA ERwin Data Modeler*. Bradley Beach, New Jersey: Technics Publications, 2011.

[Chen-1976] PPS Chen. The entity-relationship model—toward a unified view of data. *ACM Transactions on Database Systems 1*, 1 March 1976.

[Elmasri-2011] Ramez Elmasri and Shamkant B. Navathe. *Fundamentals of Database Systems, Sixth Edition*. Boston: Addison-Wesley, 2011.

[Hernandez-2013] Michael J. Hernandez. *Database Design for Mere Mortals: A Hands-On Guide to Relational Database Design, Third Edition*. Boston: Addison-Wesley, 2013.

[Hoberman-2009] Steve Hoberman. *Data Modeling Made Simple, Second Edition*. Bradley Beach, New Jersey: Technics Publications, 2009.

[OMG] The Object Management Group. www.omg.org

[Rumbaugh-2005] James Rumbaugh, Ivar Jacobson, and Grady Booch. *The Unified Modeling Language Reference Manual, Second Edition*. Boston: Addison-Wesley, 2005.

[Teorey-2011] Toby Teorey, Sam Lightstone, Tom Nadeau, and H.V. Jagadish. *Database Modeling and Design: Logical Design, Fifth Edition*. New York: Morgan Kaufmann, 2011.

2

A Data Modeling Example

This chapter presents a sample data model and explains its meaning. Subsequent chapters discuss UML and IE* modeling constructs and use portions of the example for illustration.

2.1 UML Data Model

Figure 2.1 shows a sample UML data model for an online retail Web site. Online retail is targeted at *Customers*. Each *Customer* has a name (*customerName*) as well as a *loginName* and password (*encryptedPassword*) for identification. A *Customer* can place many *Orders* and an *Order* is specific to a *Customer*.

Each *Order* has a unique *orderNumber*, as well as an *orderDateTime*, *shippingMethod* (post office, UPS, Fed Ex), *taxAmount*, *shippingHandlingAmount*, and *totalAmount*. An *Order* may have a different *shipping Address* and *billing Address*. There can be multiple *Payments* for an *Order*; each *Payment* can be by a credit card, a check, money order, or some other *paymentType*. An *Order* may consist of multiple *OrderItems*, each of which is identified by an *itemNumber* within an *Order*. Each *OrderItem* has a *quantity* of one or more.[†]

An *OrderItem* pertains to a *VendedProduct*. A *VendedProduct* is a *Product* sold by a particular *Merchant*. The *price* of a *Product* can vary by *Merchant* and *condition* (such as new, good condition, and worn).

Retail Web sites support a wide range of *Products*, of which the model shows three kinds: *Book*, *Electronics*, and *Automotive*. Many additional kinds of *Product* are possible (*OtherProduct*). The model shows some details for *Book* — the *ISBN*, *publishedDate*, *format* (hardcover or softcover), *publisherName*, and *language*. A *Book* can have multiple *Authors*,

---

* Please note: In this book IE is an acronym for Information Engineering (and not Internet Explorer).

† The relationship type between *Order* and *OrderItem* is a qualified association. The qualifier is *itemNumber*. The qualified association indicates that the combination of an *Order* and an *itemNumber* denotes a single *OrderItem*. See Chapter 7 for further explanation.

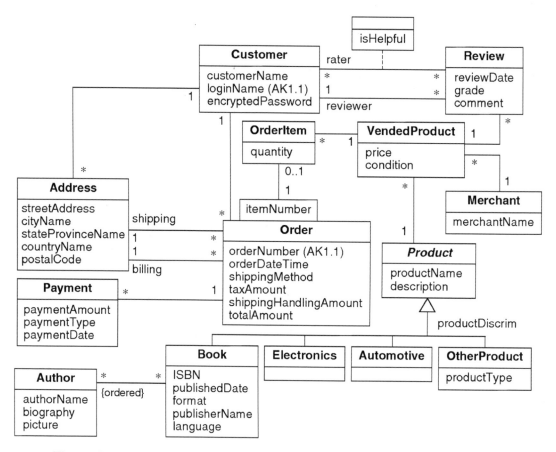

Figure 2.1 An example of a UML logical data model. This model provides
the basis for most UML examples throughout the book.

ordered by their significance. *Authors* can post information about themselves, including their
name (*authorName*), *biography*, and *picture*.

Customers can not only place *Orders*, but they can also submit *Reviews* for *VendedProducts*. In addition a *Customer* can rate someone else's *Review* and indicate if it *isHelpful*.

In business discussions, we often use the UML notation as we have here, without prior
explanation. Most business staff find the UML to be intuitive and understandable. During interactive sessions, they guide the content of a model with a modeling expert leading the way.
The modeling sessions have the side benefit of causing different departments to speak to each
other and agree on application requirements and scope. See [Blaha-2011] for a demonstration
of interactive UML data modeling.

2.2 IE Data Model

Figure 2.2 is the counterpart to Figure 2.1 and shows an IE data model for online retail. This
is just one of several IE models that correspond to the UML model. That is because an IE
model incorporates decisions about primary keys, of which there are multiple choices. In
contrast, a UML model defers database details to later development stages.

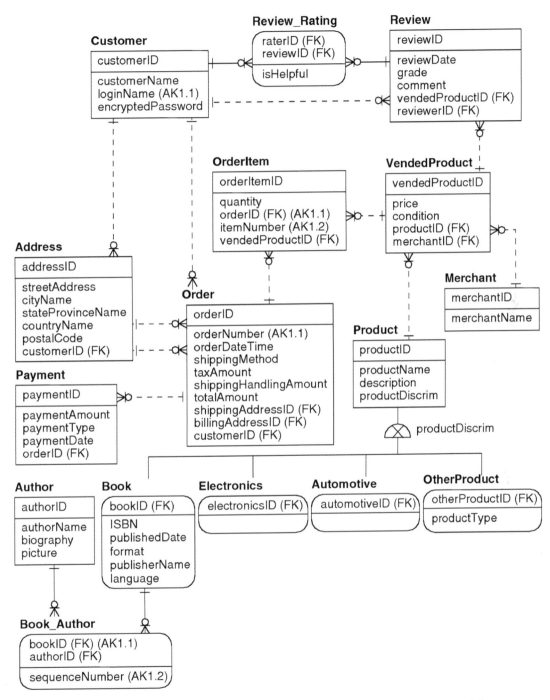

Figure 2.2 An example of an IE logical data model. This model provides
the basis for most IE examples throughout the book.

In the IE model, we named an entity type *Review_Rating*. The name for this entity type
was not needed in the UML model, but we had to create a name for it in the IE model.

2.3　Chapter Summary

A data model of customer orders for an online retail Web site provides an example of UML and IE constructs for subsequent chapters.

Bibliographic Notes

[Blaha–2005], [Fowler–2003], [Rumbaugh–2005], and [OMG] have further information about the UML notation. The UML class model is a derivative of Peter Chen's seminal ER notation and is essentially an ER dialect. The original IE books [Information Engineering] are dated now, but information about IE is available on the Web.

References

[Blaha-2005] Michael Blaha and James Rumbaugh. *Object-Oriented Modeling and Design with UML, Second Edition.* Upper Saddle River, NJ: Prentice Hall, 2005.

[Blaha-2011] A series of YouTube videos show how to construct UML data models using agile techniques. http://www.youtube.com/view_play_list?p=EE77921A75E846EB

[Chen-1976] P.P.S. Chen. The Entity-Relationship model—toward a unified view of data. *ACM Transactions on Database Systems 1*, 1 (March 1976), 9–36.

[Fowler-2003] Martin Fowler. *UML Distilled: A Brief Guide to the Standard Object Modeling Language, Third Edition.* Boston: Addison-Wesley, 2003.

[Information Engineering] Information Engineering (IE) is a database notation that was popularized by James Martin and Clive Finkelstein in the 1980s.

[OMG] The Object Management Group. www.omg.org

[Rumbaugh-2005] James Rumbaugh, Ivar Jacobson, and Grady Booch. *The Unified Modeling Language Reference Manual, Second Edition.* Boston: Addison-Wesley, 2005.

Part I

Basic Modeling Concepts

Part 1 covers basic modeling concepts — the minimal concepts that you will need to be able to start constructing UML data models. The UML has many modeling notations, of which one — the class model — is pertinent for data models. The major concepts in the class model are class, association, and generalization.

Chapter 3 presents basic class concepts. A class describes a group of objects with similar properties, behavior, relationships, and semantic intent. Classes can have attributes and operations. An attribute is a named property of a class that describes a value held by each object of the class. An operation is a function or procedure that can be applied to or by objects in a class.

Chapter 4 covers basic association concepts. An association relates classes and describes a connection among the objects of the classes. Multiplicity specifies the number of occurrences of one class that may relate to a single occurrence of an associated class. The most common combinations of multiplicity are one-to-one, one-to-many, and many-to-many. IE realizes associations via identifying and non-identifying relationship types.

Chapter 5 explains generalization, which couples a class (the superclass) to one or more variations of the class (the subclasses). Generalization organizes classes by their similarities and differences, structuring the description of objects. The superclass holds common data and the subclasses add specific data. A generalization hierarchy can extend for multiple levels.

Please work the exercises as you read the book and hold on to them. Later exercises will build on exercises that were done previously. The exercises reinforce the text and illustrate subtleties that are difficult to explain. Once you finish Part 1, you should take the self-assessment test and determine if you have mastered the material.

3

Basic Class Concepts

The class model describes data structure and is the UML model that is most relevant to databases. Classes provide the starting point for constructing class models.

3.1 Class

An *object* is a concept, abstraction, or thing that has identity and meaning for an application. A UML object corresponds to an IE entity.[*] An object is in or out of scope for a model, depending on its relevance to an application.

Application needs also determine the level of abstraction for representing an object. For example, an airplane flight can be represented by a departure/arrival time, a sequence of phases (at gate, boarding, taking off, enroute, landing, at gate, disembarking), or even more finely grained as a series of ground maneuvers and flight routes. These three representations correspond to different applications (flight departure/arrival board, flight status on a Web site, and air traffic control).

A *class* describes a group of objects with similar properties (attributes), behavior, relationships to other objects, and semantic intent. The UML symbol for a class is a box with the name of the class in the top portion of the box. In Figure 2.1 *Customer*, *Order*, and *Product* are examples of classes. Figure 2.1 has fourteen classes in total (all the boxes except *itemNumber* and *isHelpful*).

Figure 3.1 shows UML and IE notation side by side. A UML class corresponds to an IE entity type. The IE notation for an entity type is a box with the name of the entity type above the box. By convention we use a singular name for classes and capitalize the first letter.

IE distinguishes between independent and dependent entity types, based on whether identity propagates across a relationship type. (In contrast the UML has no notion of independent vs. dependent for a class.) In IE, a square box denotes an independent entity type, and a rounded box denotes a dependent entity type. The next chapter discusses relationships and elaborates.

---

[*] The literature has inconsistent meanings for the term *entity*. Sometimes an entity refers to an occurrence. Other times it refers to a descriptor for occurrences. In this book, entity always refers to an occurrence. Entity type refers to a descriptor.

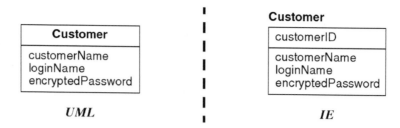

Figure 3.1 Notation for class / entity type. A class describes a group of objects with similar properties, behavior, relationships to other objects, and semantic intent

Exercises 3.1 through 3.4 can help you check your understanding of classes.

3.2 Attribute

A *value* is a piece of data that lacks identity. (Note the contrast to an object which has identity.) An *attribute* is a named property of a class that describes a value held by each object of
the class. An attribute is a "slot" for values. The UML and IE both use the terms *value* and
attribute. A class need not have attributes to merit inclusion in a data model; some classes are
included solely for their relationship types to other classes.

Structural constructs — that is classes and relationship types — dominate data models. Attributes are of lesser importance and elaborate classes and relationship types. The second portion of the UML class box shows attribute names. In Figure 3.1, *Customer* has three attributes.

As Figure 3.1 shows, the IE notation lists attributes in both portions of the entity type
box. The top portion has primary key attributes. (A primary key uniquely identifies the records in a table. See Chapter 6.) The lower portion has the remaining data attributes. By convention, we use a singular name for attributes and lower case for the first letter. When there
are multiple words in a name, you can use mixed case (as in Figure 3.1, where a capital letter
starts each subsequent word) or separate the words with underscores.

The attribute *customerID* in Figure 3.1 is a surrogate key (a generated number that
uniquely identifies a customer. See Chapter 6.) We often give surrogate key names a suffix
of *ID*.

As Figure 3.2 shows, each attribute can have an *attribute multiplicity* that specifies the
number of possible values for each record. The most common UML options are a mandatory
single value [1], an optional single value [0..1], and many [*]. Attribute multiplicity specifies
if an attribute is optional or mandatory (null or not null). It also indicates if an attribute is single valued or can be a collection. Normally, a relational database attribute cannot store a collection of values[†], but the UML permits multivalues. For IE, we had to convert the "many"
multiplicity to a relationship type which the following chapter explains. If you omit attribute
multiplicity, the UML defaults to a single value with nullability unspecified ([0..1] or [1]).

You can verify your understanding of attributes with Exercises 3.5 through 3.7.

---

† Some relational databases support complex data types, which can include collec-
tions of values. Such data types are not widely used.

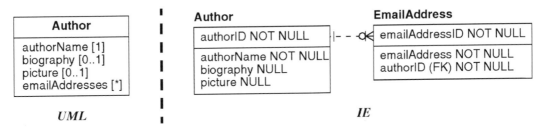

Figure 3.2 Notation for attribute multiplicity. Attribute multiplicity specifies the number of possible values.

3.3 Operation

An *operation* is a function or procedure that can be applied to or by objects in a class. IE models lack operations. Figure 3.3 adds the following operations for the online retail application. The third portion of the UML class box displays operation names:

- **addItem** — add an *OrderItem* to an *Order* and set the *itemNumber* and *quantity*.
- **editCustomerAddress** — assign an *Address* to a *Customer* and try to ensure that it does not duplicate an existing *Address* for that *Customer*.
- **editOrderAddress** — let the *Customer* edit the *shipping* and/or *billing Address* for an *Order*.
- **makePayment** — add a *Payment* record for an *Order*. Check that the *Payment* does not cause the total *paymentAmount* to exceed the *totalAmount* of the *Order*.
- **placeOrder** — indicate that a *Customer* has finished adding *OrderItems* to an *Order*.
- **postReview** — add a *Review* of a *VendedProduct* by a *Customer*. Make sure that there are no prior *Reviews* of the *VendedProduct* by the *Customer*.
- **rateReview** — comment on the helpfulness of a *Review* by a *Customer* other than the posting *Customer*.

There are several reasons for adding operations to data models:

- **Major business functionality**. A UML operation summarizes business logic and assigns it to a class. It is sometimes helpful to see a summary of functionality placed in context with the model of data structure.
- **Stored procedures**. Database stored procedures can implement operations. Stored procedures often run faster than programming code since they operate within the database kernel. Furthermore many stored procedures are interpreted, making them easier to extend and maintain than compiled programming code. See [Blaha-2006] and [Blaha-2008] for examples.
- **XSD files**. We use data models to design XSD files. XSD files specify data structure for XML files that store data occurrences. XSD files are often used as interfaces for SOA (the Service-Oriented Architecture) and operations can summarize SOA services. The functionality in Figure 3.3 could be delivered as SOA services.

Exercise 3.8 gives you practice with adding operations to a model.

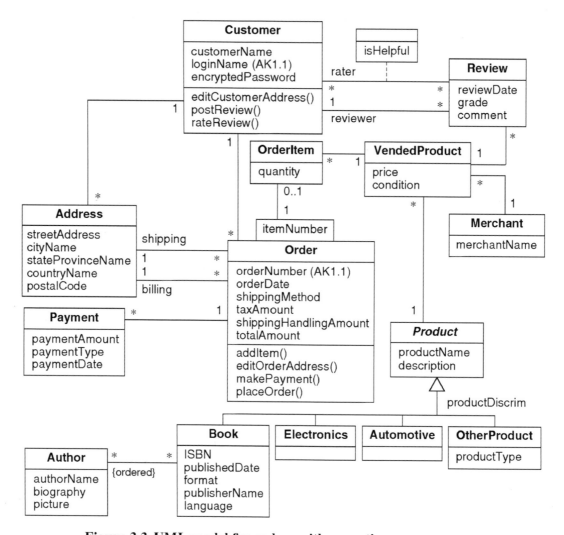

Figure 3.3 UML model for orders with operations

3.4 Domain and Data Type

A *domain* is the named set of possible values for an attribute. It is good database practice for developers to assign each attribute a domain and then separately resolve the domain to a data type. A *data type* specifies the type and size for values of the attribute to which the data type is assigned. Examples of domains include *identifier*, *name*, *amount*, *code*, and *description*. Examples of data types include long integer, varchar (20), and date. Domains provide several benefits:

- **Consistent data types**. Most domains apply to multiple attributes; therefore domains provide a mechanism for assigning consistent data types. For example, all attributes with the *name* domain would have the same data type and length and need not be assigned a data type individually.

- **Fewer decisions**. Because domains standardize data types, there are fewer implementation decisions. Data models have fewer domains than attributes.

- **Extensibility**. Data types are easier to change when similar attributes are grouped together and data types are not directly assigned.

- **Domain constraints**. A domain not only specifies a data type, but can also be used as a basis for constraints. For example, an amount must be greater than zero; a shipping method has the possible values of post office, UPS, and Fed Ex.

IE tools support domains, but most UML tools do not. Most UML tools directly assign each attribute a data type. Nevertheless, developers can still think in terms of domains.

Figure 3.4 shows notation. The UML notation lists the attribute name, a colon, the data type, and attribute multiplicity. The IE notation lists the attribute name, a colon, the domain (optional), the data type (optional, can appear with or without the domain), and nullability.

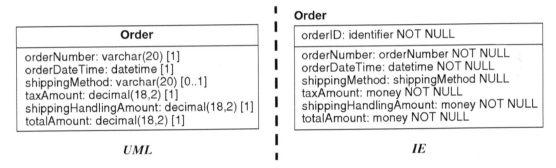

Figure 3.4 Notation for data type (UML) and domain (IE). Even when there is a lack of support, UML developers can think in terms of domains (as evident in the consistent data type and size of the *Amount* attributes).

Some domains are enumerations. An **enumeration domain** limits attribute values to a list of choices. In Figure 3.4, *shippingMethod* is an enumeration domain with the possible values of post office, UPS, or Fed Ex. Other domains concern numbers (such as *money* in Figure 3.4), strings (such as *orderNumber* in Figure 3.4), *datetime*, and miscellaneous data.

You can check your understanding of domains with Exercise 3.9.

3.5 Definitions

As you construct models, it is important to document them. At a minimum, make sure you define all major classes — the classes that are prominent in an application.

One way to document models is by writing a narrative. We copy and paste model diagrams into a document and then explain them. Then customers can see the model and explanation without needing access to a modeling tool. The downside of this approach is that the documentation becomes stale as a model evolves and requires periodic update.

Alternatively, you can document a model by preparing a data dictionary. A **data dictionary** is a list of definitions for important concepts. A good definition should explain the intrinsic nature of a concept along with any subtleties, assumptions, and important constraints. Most data modeling tools can bind a definition to a model construct. These definitions endure as a model is updated and concepts are renamed. The downside of this approach is that it can be awkward to see definitions without access to the modeling tool.

Here are definitions for the major classes in the online retail example:

- **Customer**. A person with a login name and password. Ideally a person should have no more than one customer record, but some multiples will occur. Each order is for a customer and a customer can have zero or more orders. A customer may post reviews and review ratings.

- **Order**. A request for one or more vended products. The model says that an order has zero or more items, but in reality, an order must have at least one item. (With a database, it is awkward to enforce an order having at least one item.)

- **OrderItem**. A request for some quantity of a vended product within an order. The model permits the same vended product to appear multiple times (as separate items) in the same order. Application software would probably keep this from occurring, even though there is no database enforcement. Items are assigned a unique item number within an order.

- **Product**. A good for sale. We exclude services from the scope of online retailing.

- **Review**. An opinion about a vended product by a customer. We assume that reviews are automatically posted and are not vetted.

- **VendedProduct**. A product that is provided by a specific merchant. A product may have multiple vended products for the same merchant, especially if the vended products are in different conditions.

You can check your understanding of definitions with Exercise 3.10.

3.6 Practical Tips

Consider the following tips as you construct models:

- **Scope**. Make sure you clearly understand the problem to be solved. The content of a data model is driven by application needs. For example, the online retail application covers the scope of servicing customer orders.

- **Business rationale**. Don't build a model without understanding the business rationale. The purpose dictates the level of polish, the degree of completeness, and the amount of time justified. For example, development requires a detailed application model with attributes and domains. A high-level model can suffice as a purchase specification or as a guide for enterprise integration.

- **Names**. Carefully choose names. Names carry powerful connotations. Names should be descriptive, crisp, and unambiguous. When struggling with a name, I've found that a clear definition often suggests what the name should be. Therefore, naming and definitions should go hand-in-hand. How do you know you've named something properly if you can't define it?. Users often argue over names, but the arguments can be worthwhile because they cause deep thinking about a model and help forge a consensus.

- **Lexicon**. It is a good idea to standardize rules for naming, especially for a large model.

- **Operations**. Consider adding operation names to your data models to document high-level functionality.
- **Domains**. Specify domains for attributes instead of data types. Domains promote uniform assignment of data types and provide a hook for attaching constraints.
- **Enumerations**. Declare enumerations and their values because they often occur and are important to users.
- **Documentation**. Always document your models and define terminology. The diagram specifies a model's structure but cannot describe the rationale. A written explanation can guide the reader and explain subtle model decisions.

3.7 Chapter Summary

An object is a concept, abstraction, or thing that has identity and meaning for an application. A class describes a group of objects with similar attributes, behavior, relationships to other objects, and semantic intent.

A value is a piece of data that lacks identity. An attribute is a named property of a class that describes a value held by each object of the class. An attribute is a "slot" for values. Attribute multiplicity specifies if an attribute is single or multivalued and if it is optional or mandatory (null or not null). An operation is a function or procedure that can be applied to or by objects in a class.

A domain is the named set of possible values for an attribute. Good database practice is to use domains to organize the assignment of data types.

Table 3.1 summarizes UML and IE concepts.

UML Concept	UML Notation	IE Concept	IE Notation	Definition
Object		Entity		A concept, abstraction, or thing that has identity and meaning for an application.
Class	▭	Entity type	▭	A group of objects with similar attributes, behavior, relationships to other objects, and semantic intent.
Value		Value		A piece of data that lacks identity.
Attribute	▤	Attribute	▤ ⬭	A named property of a class that describes a value held by each object of the class.
Operation	▤			A function or procedure that can be applied to or by objects in a class.
		Domain		The named set of possible values for an attribute.
Data type		Data type		A specification of type and size for values such as long integer, varchar(20), and date.

Table 3.1 Terminology summary

Bibliographic Notes

[Blaha-2006] has a detailed data model with operations and an implementation with SQL Server stored procedures. [Blaha-2008] provides guidance for implementing operations with SQL Server stored procedures.

Sometimes there is a need to couple object-oriented programming to a database. An object-oriented programming class can map to an entity type or to a domain. A lightweight class (such as *name*, *amount*, or *code*) maps to a domain. A substantive class (an application class, such as *Customer* or *Product*) maps to an entity type.

The origins of the UML class model lie in the ER model [Chen-1976]. The UML class model is essentially just an ER dialect (albeit one with programming jargon that is not relevant to databases).

References

[Blaha-2006] Michael Blaha. Designing and Implementing Softcoded Values. *IEEE Computer Society ReadyNote*, 2006.

[Blaha-2008] Michael Blaha, Bill Huth, and Peter Cheung. Object-Oriented Design of Database Stored Procedures. www.odbms.org/download/007.04%20Blaha%20Object-Oriented%20Design%20of%20Database%20Stored%20Procedures%20October%202008.PDF

[Chen-1976] P.P.S. Chen. The Entity-Relationship model—toward a unified view of data. *ACM Transactions on Database Systems 1*, 1 (March 1976), 9–36.

Exercises

Each exercise has a difficulty level ranging from 1 (easy) to 10 (very difficult).

3.1 (3) Prepare a list of classes that you would expect for a database of scores and statistics for baseball games. List at least six classes.

3.2 (3) Find tentative classes for the requirements in Figure E3.1. List at least six classes.

> Develop software for managing a health spa. For simplicity, you can assume a single spa location with a fixed number of rooms. The spa employs multiple therapists, some of whom are working at any time during business hours. The therapists perform treatments from a predefined list. Each treatment is performed for a single customer, on a date for some time duration, for one room, and by one therapist.
>
> The software must be able to schedule appointments by finding the available time slots for a room, as well as the available time slots for a therapist. Some customers have a preference for a particular therapist and favored treatments that must be noted. The system also must record the revenue from each treatment that is performed. A treatment has a list price, but there can be discounts.

Figure E3.1 Requirements for software for managing a health spa

3.3 (3) Find tentative classes for the requirements in Figure E3.2. List at least six classes.

Prepare a simple UML model for online auctions. Your model should emphasize the needs of auction bidders rather than sellers.

The listings for online auctions consist of many auction items. Each auction item has a seller and any number of bids from various bidders. An auction item has a number, description, closing date and time, reserve price, handling cost, shipping cost, current price, payment method, and currency. Both buyers and sellers can leave feedback after an auction of an item, expressing their satisfaction or dissatisfaction. A feedback comment may be subject to a reply. Auction items are organized into categories that have a hierarchical structure.

Figure E3.2 Requirements for online auctions

3.4 (8) Figure E3.3 shows an excerpt of a restaurant menu. List at least four classes. Hint: Your answer should abstract the data in the menu.

Sombrero Mexican Restaurant — Dinner Menu

Appetizers

- Chicken quesadilla — with grilled onions & peppers served with guacamole, salsa, & sour cream — $6.00
- Beef nachos — crispy homemade corn chips, served with guacamole, salsa & sour cream — $5.00 (small), $8.00 (large)
- Soup du jour — $4.00

Salads

- House salad — your choice of dressing (french, bleu cheese, ranch, balsamic vinaigrette, honey mustard) — $5.00
- Caesar salad — anchovies upon request — $5.00

Entrees

- Beef tamales — $8.95
- Chile rellenos — stuffed pepper with ground beef or cheese — $8.50
- Burritos — beef $8.75   chicken $8.25   bean $7.95   veggie $6.95
- Tacos — your choice of beef or chicken / hard or soft — $8.75

Beverages

- Coffee — $1.50
- Tea — hot or iced — $1.50
- Soda — cola, root beer, lemon-lime — $1.50

Figure E3.3 Excerpt of a sample restaurant menu

3.5 (5) Consider a TV guide database that holds listings about programs on TV. Which of the following are classes and which are attributes? Assign attributes to their corresponding class. Explain your decisions. See www.tvguide.com/listings for further examples.

- network. Examples: ABC, CBS, FOX, Telemundo.

- program. Examples: General Hospital, Let's Make a Deal, Local Programming, Remember the Titans.
- listing. Example: General Hospital is a program. The ABC showing on May 2, 2012 at 3 PM EDT is a listing.
- program name. Examples: The string "General Hospital", the string "Local Programming".
- new or repeat. A program is new the first time it is shown (a listing). It is a repeat subsequent times that it is shown (more listings).
- listing date. Example: May 2, 2012.
- start time. Example: 3 PM.
- duration. Example: 1 hour.
- program category. Examples: movies, sports, family, news.
- synopsis. Example: A football coach tries to promote racial harmony among the players of a newly integrated high-school squad in early 1970s Virginia.
- year released. Example: 2000.
- director. Example: Boaz Yakin.
- actor/actress. Examples: Denzel Washington, Will Patton, Wood Harris, Ryan Hurst.
- carrier. Examples: Comcast, Charter, DirectTV.
- channel. Examples: 2, 4, 5.
- rating. Examples: PG, PG-MA, R, X.
- rating reason. This is a brief explanation of the reason for the rating, such as L for language or N for nudity.

3.6 (4) Figure E3.4 shows a simple model for an auto dealer Web site. (This exercise illustrates the use of underscores.) Assign each of the following attributes to one or more classes.

body_style, condition, fuel_efficiency, list_price, mileage, name, stock_number, year

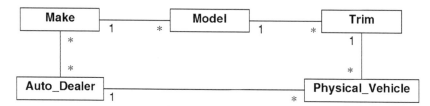

Figure E3.4 Classes for a simple model of an auto dealer Web site

The following examples clarify terminology:
- Make. Examples: Toyota, Chevrolet, Ford.
- Model. Examples: Camry, Corrolla, Prius.
- Trim. Examples: 4 door sedan L4 auto LE, 4 door sedan V6 auto SE.
- body_style. Examples: sedan, hatchback, convertible, van.

3.7 (5) Figure E3.5 shows a model for educational courses. In the model, *Location* is a class room or a URL. Assign each of the following attributes to one or more classes.

code, creditHours, dayOfWeek, description, endDate, endTime, grade, name, registrationDate, sectionNumber, semester, startDate, startTime, withdrawDate, year

3.8 (6) Add the following operations to the answer for the prior exercise. Define the operations.

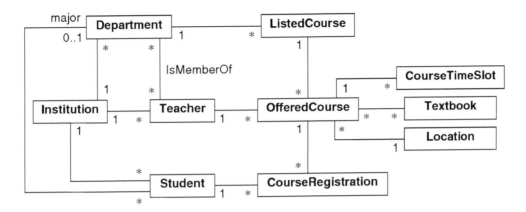

Figure E3.5 Classes for an educational course model

addListedcourse, dropListedCourse, dropStudent, dropStudentForCourse, postGrade, register-Student, registerStudentForCourse, scheduleOfferedCourse

3.9   (3) Add domains to each of the attributes from the answer to Exercise 3.6.

3.10 (5) Prepare a data dictionary for the classes in Exercise 3.7.

4

Basic Association Concepts

Associations provide the means for relating classes. Associations are a prominent feature of the UML and are especially helpful for modeling databases.

4.1 Association

4.1.1 UML

A *link* is a physical or conceptual connection among objects. An ***association*** describes a group of links with common structure and semantics. An association describes a set of potential links in the same way that a class describes a set of potential objects. A UML link corresponds to an IE relationship and a UML association corresponds to an IE relationship type.[*]

The UML notation for an association is a line (possibly with multiple line segments) that connects the related classes. The line between *Customer* and *Address* in Figure 4.1 is an association.

4.1.2 IE

Figure 4.1 also shows IE notation. IE distinguishes between identifying and non-identifying relationship types, as well as independent and dependent entity types. IE shows relationship types redundantly with lines and (FK – foreign key) annotation.

An ***identifying relationship type*** propagates primary key[†] attributes of the source entity type (*Customer* in Figure 4.1) to the primary key of the referent entity type (*Address* in Figure

---

[*] The literature has inconsistent meanings for the term *relationship*. Sometimes a relationship refers to an occurrence. Other times it refers to a descriptor. In this book, relationship denotes an occurrence, and relationship type denotes a descriptor.

[†] A primary key uniquely identifies each record in a table and is used for internal table references. A foreign key is a reference to a unique identifier of a related table (usually the primary key of the related table).

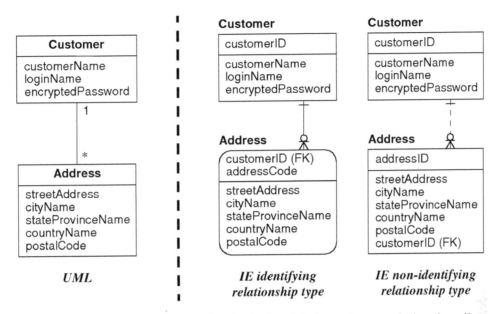

Figure 4.1 Notation for association / relationship type. An association describes a group of links with common structure and semantics.

4.1). A solid line connects the entity types. The referent entity type is necessarily dependent (rounded box).

A ***non-identifying relationship type*** propagates primary key attributes of the source entity type (*Customer* in Figure 4.1) to data attributes of the referent entity type (*Address* in Figure 4.1). A dashed line connects the entity types. The referent entity type may be independent (square box) or dependent (rounded box) depending on its other relationship types and generalizations (next chapter).

As Figure 4.2 shows, an IE relationship type line (whether solid or dashed) can be positioned so that it touches the entity type box (left model), but it need not (right model).

An ***independent entity type*** does not include any foreign keys in its primary key. Some authors call this a ***strong entity type***. The IE symbol is a square-corner box. An independent entity type can only have foreign keys from non-identifying relationship types.

A ***dependent entity type*** includes one or more foreign keys in its primary key (via one or more identifying relationship types or via generalization, see the next chapter). It can exist only if one or more other entity types also exist. Some authors call this a ***weak entity type***. The IE symbol is a rounded box.

IE represents many-to-many relationship types with a dependent entity type and two or more identifying relationship types. *Review_Rating* in Figure 4.3 is an example and is called an ***associative entity type***. An associative entity type obtains its primary key from two or more other entity types. *Review_Rating.raterID* refers to *Customer.customerID*; see Section 4.3 for explanation.

Exercises 4.1 through 4.6 can help you check your understanding of associations.

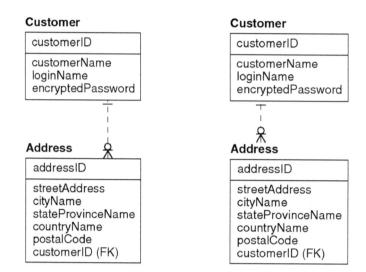

Figure 4.2 IE relationship type. An IE relationship type line may touch the entity type box (left model), but it need not (right model).

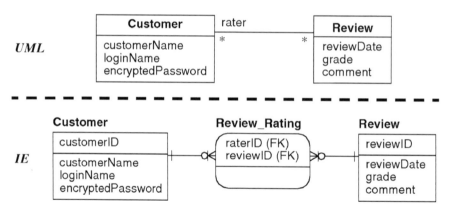

Figure 4.3 IE associative entity type. An associative entity type obtains its primary key from two or more other entity types.

4.2 Association Name

Figure 2.1 omits association names. Figure 4.4 shows a model excerpt with association names. The UML only requires association names (or end names, see Section 4.3) when there are multiple associations between the same classes. Regardless, you are free to name associations, if you prefer.

As Figure 4.4 shows, an association name often reads in a particular direction. Nevertheless, associations can be traversed either way. Thus, given a *shipping Address*, we can find the associated *Orders*. Given an *Order* we can find the associated *shipping Address*. This association traversal is analogous to combining relational database tables via foreign-key-to-primary-key joins.

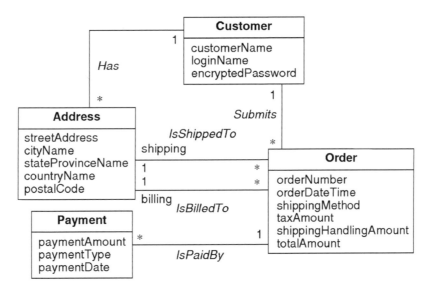

Figure 4.4 UML model with association names. Association
names are optional if a model is unambiguous.

It is a common IE practice to include relationship type names. Each relationship type can have either a single name or a pair of directed names (Figure 4.5). A single name can be useful for development (it provides a table name). Directed names add bulk but make a model more readable. As mentioned earlier, the UML can assign an association name. The UML also has a navigation icon to show the direction for reading the name (not shown here), but the UML has no pairing of association names for reading in each direction.

Exercises 4.7 and 4.8 can help you confirm your understanding of association names.

4.3 Association End

An *association end name* is an alias for a class in an association. The UML notation is a legend next to the class–association intersection.[‡]

Association end names are optional if a model is unambiguous. As Figure 4.6 shows, ambiguity occurs when there are multiple associations for the same classes (*Address* and *Order*) or an association for objects of the same class (*Person*). You have a choice of association names or end names to resolve multiple associations for the same classes. You must use end names to clarify an association for objects of the same class. Regardless of ambiguity, you are always free to use association names and end names to annotate a model.

When constructing models, you should properly use association ends and not introduce a separate class for each reference. For example, an inferior model would have *Mother* and *Father* as classes.

Association end names are more profound than association names. Figure 4.7 summarizes the benefits.

---

‡ UML 1.0 used the term *role*. UML 2.0 now uses the term *association end*.

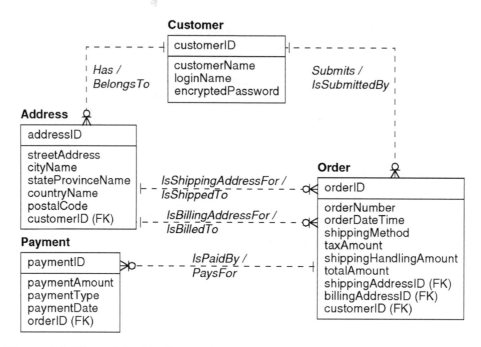

Figure 4.5 IE model with directed names. You can assign a pair of directed
names to a relationship type. The top name reads from the 'one' entity
type to the 'many' entity type and vice versa for the bottom name.

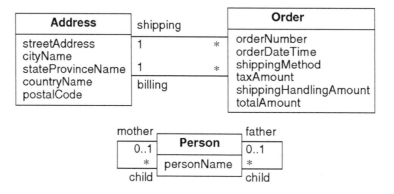

Figure 4.6 UML association end names. Association end names
can resolve ambiguity.

An end name is a pseudo attribute because of its eventual implementation with a database
foreign key. Since it is a pseudo attribute, an end name must not clash with any other attribute
or end name of the origination class. For example, in Figure 4.6, the *Order* table would include the six listed attributes, as well as the shipping and billing address — all eight attributes
must be distinct.**

** There is also a ninth attribute, *orderID*, given our approach to identity.

Benefits of association names:

- Improves model readability.
- Provides a table name for an associative entity type.
- Disambiguates multiple associations for the same classes.

Benefits of association end names:

- Improves model readability.
- Provides a foreign key name.
- Disambiguates multiple associations for the same classes.
- Disambiguates an association for objects of the same class.
- Provides clarity for model traversal and SQL queries.

Figure 4.7 Association name vs. association end name. Association
end names are more profound than association names.

As Figure 4.8 illustrates, IE can indicate role names with a dot notation. (Alternatively, you can just show the role name and omit the reference, which is *shippingAddressID* rather than *shippingAddressID.addressID*). IE roles are the counterpart to UML association ends. (Figure 4.8 corresponds to Figure 4.6.)

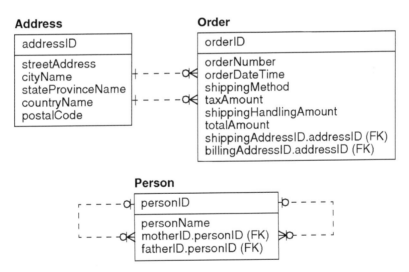

Figure 4.8 IE roles. An IE role corresponds to a UML association end.

You can verify your understanding of association ends with Exercises 4.9 and 4.12.

4.4 Multiplicity

Multiplicity specifies the number of occurrences of one class that may relate to a single occurrence of an associated class. Thus multiplicity pertains to an association end. The most common multiplicities are "1", "0..1", and "*" (the special symbol for "many" — zero or more). Figure 4.9 shows examples. A *Customer* can perform many *Reviews* and a *Review* is from one *reviewer Customer* (a one-to-many association). A *Customer* can rate many *Reviews* and a *Review* may have many *rater Customers* (a many-to-many association).

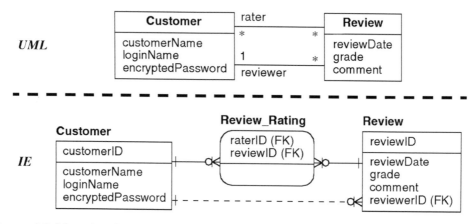

Figure 4.9 Notation for multiplicity. Multiplicity specifies the number of occurrences of one class that may relate to a single occurrence of an associated class

Much of the database literature incorrectly uses the term *cardinality*, instead of the proper term *multiplicity*. Multiplicity is a constraint on the size of a collection; cardinality is the count of elements that are actually in a collection. Therefore, multiplicity is a constraint on the cardinality.

Figure 4.10 compares UML and IE multiplicity notation. The IE representation depends on the choice of primary key and use of identifying vs. non-identifying relationship types. IE uses a small circle, vertical bar, and a "crow's foot" to denote "many" multiplicity (zero or more). A small circle and vertical bar denote "at most one" multiplicity (zero or one). A small vertical bar indicates a multiplicity of exactly one. There are additional possible combinations of multiplicity that Figure 4.10 does not show, but they seldom occur.

For each association there is at most one link between a given pair of objects. Thus, a *shippingAddress* can be associated with *Order 1234* at most once; if the *shippingAddress* has additional *Order* objects, they must be different from *1234*, and all must be distinct. Figure 4.11 emphasizes this point. If you want two links between the same objects, you must have two associations.

Minimum multiplicity is the lower limit on the possible number of related objects. The most common values are zero and one. A minimum multiplicity of zero permits null values, and a minimum multiplicity of one forbids null values. (*Null* is a special value denoting that an attribute value is unknown or not applicable.) A minimum multiplicity of one implies an existence dependency between objects.

Maximum multiplicity is the upper limit on the possible number of related objects. The most common values are one and infinite.

You can check your understanding of multiplicity with Exercises 4.9 through 4.12.

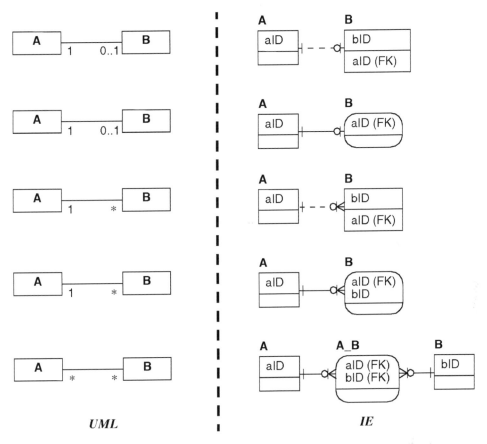

Figure 4.10 Notation for multiplicity. The UML and IE have notation
for common multiplicities.

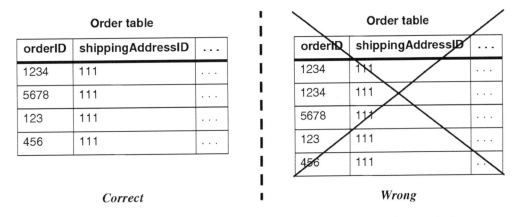

Figure 4.11 The meaning of "many" multiplicity. For each association
there is at most one link between a given pair of objects.

4.5 Analogies

Link, object, and value are occurrences. Association, class, and attribute are descriptors. The following analogies hold: link is to association as object is to class as value is to attribute.

An object is different from a link. An object has intrinsic identity. In contrast, a link is identified by some combination of participating objects. An object exists in its own right. A link exists only if its constituent objects exist. A link depends on its objects, but it is not part of any object.

A value is also different from a link. A value is a primitive, such as a number, date, or string. A link is a dependency among objects and is implemented by databases with foreign keys. A foreign key refers to an object and has more stature than a mere value.

4.6 Practical Tips

Consider the following tips as you construct models:

- **Names**. Use association names and/or end names to resolve multiple associations for the same classes. Use association end names to resolve an association for objects of the same class. You are always free to use association names and end names, especially where they add clarity and meaning to a model.

- **Association ends**. An association end is the use of a class in an association; a class may have various association ends. Do not introduce multiple classes when there really is just one class with multiple uses. It is a good practice to label a class with its intrinsic name.

- **Multiplicity**. Scrutinize association ends with a multiplicity of one. Sometimes the object is optional and zero-or-one multiplicity may be more appropriate. Other times "many" multiplicity is needed.

- **Simplicity**. Try to simplify your models. A simple model is easier to understand and less work to develop. Don't include speculative content. If classes are difficult to define, you may need to make revisions.

4.7 Chapter Summary

A link is a physical or conceptual connection among objects. An association describes a group of links with common structure and semantics. An association describes a set of potential links in the same way that a class describes a set of potential objects.

An association end is the use of a class in an association. An association end can have a name and a multiplicity. Multiplicity specifies the number of occurrences of one class that may relate to a single occurrence of an associated class.

Table 4.1 summarizes UML and IE concepts.

Bibliographic Notes

[Hay-2012] uses UML association ends to express directed relationship types. This approach conflicts with the defined meaning of association ends. However, I am not aware of any other

UML Concept	UML Notation	IE Concept	IE Notation	Definition
Link		Relationship		A physical or conceptual connection among objects.
Association	————	Relationship type	– – – –	Describes a group of links with common structure and semantics.
Association end		Role		The use of a class in an association.
		Associative entity type		Resolves a many-to-many relationship type.
Multiplicity	1 0..1 *	Cardinality (though technically incorrect)		Specifies the number of occurrences of one class that may relate to a single occurrence of an associated class.
		Identifying relationship type	————	Propagates source primary key attributes to the referent primary key.
		Non-identifying relationship type	– – – –	Propagates source primary key attributes to referent data attributes.
		Independent entity type		Has no foreign keys in its primary key. Also called a strong entity type.
		Dependent entity type		Includes foreign key(s) in its primary key. Also called a weak entity type.

Table 4.1 Terminology summary

way to express directed relationship type names with the UML. (Hay did not use association ends in this way by mistake. Rather this was his workaround for the UML limitation.)

In this author's opinion, directed association names provide little benefit. Even with directed association names, it is difficult to read a large model. Furthermore, a developer should never disseminate a "naked" model. It is important to define terminology and explain modeling decisions. This author prefers a narrative that walks the reader through a data modeling diagram, interspersed with key definitions. Of course, it is difficult to keep a narrative consistent with an evolving model, in contrast to self-documenting directed association names. There is no perfect solution. You will have to make your own trade-offs.

A data dictionary is an alternative to a model narrative. Modern tools can tie definitions to classes / entity types and attributes. (Double click on a class / entity type or attribute and a window pops up for data entry.) A data dictionary is helpful for experienced developers, but is inadequate for business readers. Business staff often feel overwhelmed by a large diagram and need help with reading it. Most business staff also lack access to modeling tools.

[Teorey-2006] uses the term *connectivity* of a relationship type instead of multiplicity or cardinality. The authors correctly note that connectivity is a constraint on the relationship type and that cardinality is a count.

This book covers the UML concepts that are commonly needed for data modeling. We deliberately omitted aggregation (the a-part-of relationship type). Aggregation is important for some specialized applications (such as bill-of-materials). Otherwise, it seldom arises and can simply be degraded to association in the few situations where it occurs.

References

[Hay-2012] David C Hay. *UML and Data Modeling: A Reconciliation*. Westfield, New Jersey: Technics Publications, 2012.

[Teorey-2006] Toby Teorey, Sam Lightstone, and Tom Nadeau. *Database Modeling and Design, Fourth Edition*. New York: Morgan Kaufmann, 2006.

Exercises

Each exercise has a difficulty level ranging from 1 (easy) to 10 (very difficult).

4.1   (8) Start with the answer to the baseball example in Exercise 3.1 and prepare a UML model.

4.2   (3) Translate the UML answer for the prior exercise to IE. Disregard the ordering of *PlateAppearances* within an *Inning*.

4.3   (3) Figure E4.1 shows an IE model for the health spa example in Exercise 3.2. Translate the IE model to a UML model. Note the following about the model:

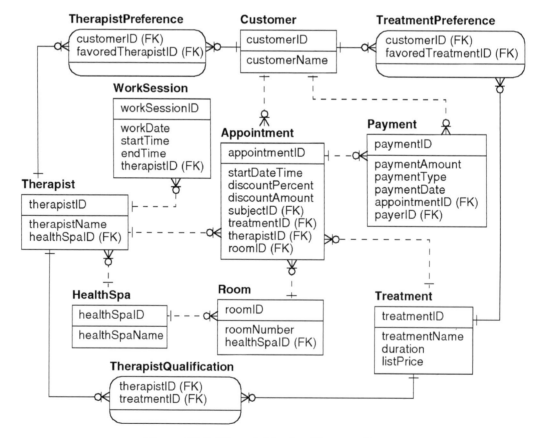

Figure E4.1 IE model for health spa software

- Only some therapists can perform particular treatments (*TherapistQualification*).

- Assume one therapist per appointment.

- Payment can be made by a different person than the subject of an appointment.

- The model considers the person making a payment also to be a customer.

- A *WorkSession* for a *Therapist* could be from 9 AM to 5 PM on March 14, 2010 while an *Appointment* for a *Customer* might be from 1 PM to 2 PM on March 14, 2010.

- There are important constraints that the model does not (and reasonably cannot) enforce.
  Appointments cannot overlap for a *Customer*.
  Appointments cannot overlap for a *Therapist*.
  Appointments cannot overlap for a *Room*.
  A *Customer Appointment* must conform to the hours of a *Therapist's WorkSession*.
  The sum of *Payment amount* cannot exceed the *Treatment listPrice* less discount.

- *TherapistPreference* and *TreatmentPreference* indicate the therapists and treatments that a *Customer* prefers.

4.4   (7) Prepare a UML model for the online auction problem in Exercise 3.3. Start with the answer to Exercise 3.3. In your model combine *Bidder* and *Seller* into a *Customer* class.

4.5   (7) Prepare a UML model for the Netflix requirements in Figure E4.2.

Netflix offers a mail-order movie rental service. The cheapest plan lets a customer have one movie at a time. When the current rental is returned, a new movie is sent. A second plan lets a customer have two movies at a time. However, the second plan limits a customer to a maximum of 4 movies per month.

Each customer has a movie request list. The movie at the top of the list is sent upon a return. If the list is empty, no movie is sent until the customer adds titles.

Netflix assigns one or more genres to each movie (science fiction, drama, etc.) and the customer can search by genre to add movies to their list. Netflix also provides movie synopses and overall customer ratings.

Each customer must provide an email address and password, as well as a credit card number for billing. Netflix sends email to customers requesting the date when the movie arrived. This helps Netflix spot delivery problems.

Figure E4.2 Requirements for Netflix software

4.6   (5) Figure E4.3 shows a model where some attributes refer to classes. Restate the model replacing these attributes with associations. Eliminate all IDs.

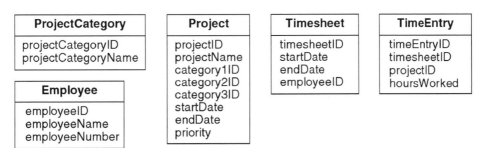

Figure E4.3 Timesheet model where some attributes refer to classes

4.7 (1) Add association names to all the associations in Figure 2.1.

4.8 (1) Add directed names to all the relationship types in Figure 2.2.

4.9 (7) Figure E4.4 shows requirements for some capabilities of the LinkedIn Web site. Prepare a UML model using the listed classes. Add associations and multiplicity from the requirements. Use association end names to disambiguate multiple associations between the same classes.

Affiliation, EmailAddress, Link, Member, Membership, MemberTagging, Tag, Title

---

Prepare a model for the LinkedIn Web site (www.linkedin.com). The model must record connectivity among members for the entire LinkedIn database. For each member store the member name, login name, encrypted password, and current e-mail addresses. Record the history for a member, that is the starting, ending, and then restarting of a membership. For each member, record past and current titles, as well as past and current affiliations.

Each member can affix tags to linked members. A tag is any string that a member defines. Tags are convenient for retrieving lists of members. Sample tags include "friend", "family", "co-worker", and "colleague". John Doe might be assigned "friend" and "family". Jane Smith might be assigned "colleague". The software should record the tags that are affixed by a member to other members.

Figure E4.4 Requirements for the LinkedIn Web site

4.10 (3) Figure E4.5 shows a model for the TV listing example in Exercise 3.5. Add multiplicity to the diagram.

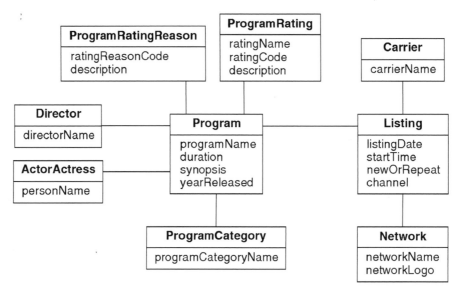

Figure E4.5 UML model for TV listings without multiplicity

4.11 (4) Figure E4.6 shows a sample auto insurance card. Figure E4.7 shows a UML model with classes and associations. Add multiplicity to the model.

Missouri Insurance Card

123 Main St   Chesterfield, MO 63017

Insured   **Doe, John J**

Policy Number   **123 4567 X89-11**   Effective
Yr **1999**   Make   **Toyota**   **Mar 14, 2012** to **Sep 14, 2012**
Model **SIENNA**   VIN **4T3ZQ14D9XU109624**
Agent **Jim Smith**   **3178-557**
Phone **(636)555-1234**   NAIC **25984**
  A   Bodily Injury/Property Damage Liability
  C   Medical Payments
  D   500 Deduct Comprehensive
  G   1000 Deduct Collision

Figure E4.6 A sample auto insurance card

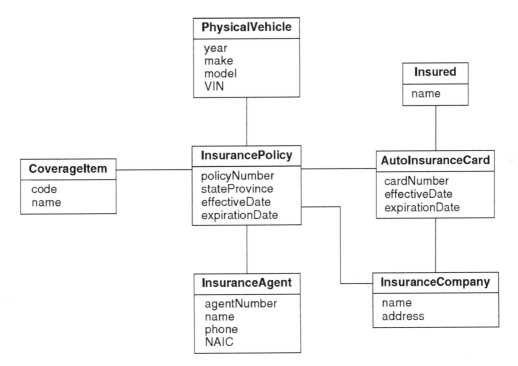

Figure E4.7 UML model for auto insurance card without multiplicity

4.12 (6) Figure E4.8 shows a U.S. customs form. Prepare a UML model using the listed classes. Add associations and multiplicity from the requirements implicit in the form. Use association end names to disambiguate multiple associations between the same classes.
  Address, Country, CustomsDeclaration, Person

U.S. Customs and Border Protection

Customs Declaration

Each arriving traveler or responsible family member must provide the following
information (only ONE written declaration per family is required):

1. Family **Name** . . . .
   First (Given) . . . .   Middle . . . .
2. **Birth date**   Day . . . . . .   Month . . . . . .   Year . . . .
3. Number of **Family members** traveling with you . . . .
4. (a) U.S. Street **Address** (hotel name / destination)
   . . . .
   (b) City . . . .   (c) State . . . .
5. **Passport issued by** (country) . . . .
6. **Passport number** . . . .
7. Country of **Residence** . . . .
8. **Countries visited** on this . . . .
   trip prior to U.S. arrival . . . .
9. **Airline / Flight No.** or **Vessel Name** . . . .
10. The primary purpose of this trip is **business** . . . . . . Yes . . . . . No . . . . . .
11. I am (We are) bringing
    (a) fruits, vegetables, plants, seeds, food, insects . . Yes . . . . . No . . . . . .
    (b) meats, animals, animal/wildlife products . . . . . Yes . . . . . No . . . . . .
    (c) disease agents, cell cultures, snails . . . . Yes . . . . . No . . . . . .
    (d) soil or have been on a farm/ranch/pasture . . . . . Yes . . . . . No . . . . . .
12. I have (We have) been in close proximity of
    (such as touching or handling) **livestock:** . . . . Yes . . . . . No . . . . . .
13. I am (We are) carrying **currency or monetary**
    instruments over $10,000 U.S. or foreign equivalent: Yes . . No . . . . . .
    (see definition of monetary instruments on reverse)
14. I have (We have) **commercial merchandise:** . . . . Yes . . . . . No . . . . . .
    (articles for sale, samples used for soliciting orders,
    or goods that are not considered personal effects)
15. **Residents** — the **total value of all goods**, including commercial
    merchandise I/we have purchased or acquired abroad, (including gifts
    for someone else, but not items mailed to the U.S.) and am/are bringing
    to the U.S. is: . . . . $ . . . .
    Visitors — the **total value of all articles** that will remain in the U.S.,
    including commercial merchandise is: . . . . $ . . . .

Read the instructions on the back of this form. Space is provided to list all the
items you must declare.

**I HAVE READ THE IMPORTANT INFORMATION ON THE REVERSE
SIDE OF THIS FORM AND HAVE MADE A TRUTHFUL DECLARATION.**

Signature . . . . Date . . . .

Figure E4.8 U.S. customs form

5

Basic Generalization Concepts

Generalization is a defining characteristic of object-oriented software approaches and organizes classes by their similarities and differences. Generalization adds to the fabric of classes and associations and enriches a modeling language. This leads to smaller models with deeper insight.

5.1 Generalization

Generalization couples a class (the superclass) to one or more variations of the class (the subclasses). The *superclass* holds common information (attributes, operations, and associations). Each *subclass* adds specific information. Generalization organizes classes by their similarities and differences, structuring the description of objects. Generalization can arise from requirements that list structural alternatives. For example, a product can be a book, electronics, automotive, or something else. In addition, modelers can introduce generalization on their own to rationalize and deepen a model's structure.

The UML notation for generalization is a large hollow arrowhead that points to the superclass. Lines fan out towards the subclasses. In Figure 5.1 *Product* is the superclass. *Book*, *Electronics*, and *Automotive* are subclasses.

The *generalization set name* (*productDiscriminator*) is an enumerated attribute that can be placed next to the generalization symbol. The generalization set name has one value for each subclass and indicates the corresponding subclass for each superclass occurrence.

Generalization has two purposes. The first is reuse; subclasses can share information that superclasses provide. The second is to structure the description of objects. Generalization lets you form a taxonomy and declare what is similar and what is different about classes. This is much more profound than modeling each class individually and in isolation. Note that generalization structures objects by similarities and differences, not by importance.

The terms generalization, specialization, and inheritance all refer to the same idea. Generalization and specialization concern class structure and take opposite perspectives. *Generalization* indicates that the superclass generalizes the subclasses. *Specialization* means that the

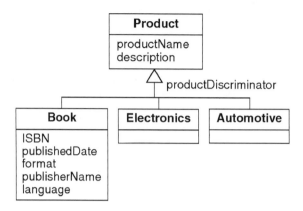

Figure 5.1 UML notation for generalization. Generalization organizes classes by
their similarities and differences, structuring the description of objects.

subclasses refine or specialize the superclass. *Inheritance* is the mechanism for sharing within
a generalization.

Simple generalization (this chapter) organizes classes into a hierarchy; each subclass has
a single immediate superclass. (Chapter 8 discusses more complex forms of generalization
in which a subclass may have multiple immediate superclasses.)

Exercises 5.1 through 5.5 can give you practice with generalization.

5.2 Abstract vs. Concrete Class

An *abstract class* is a class that has no direct occurrences. The UML indicates an abstract class
by italicizing the class name or placing the legend {abstract} before or after the class name.
A *concrete class* is a class that can have direct occurrences. The UML has no special notation
for a concrete class, just the absence of abstract class indication.

All leaf classes in a generalization are, by definition, concrete as they terminate the hierarchy. A superclass can be abstract or concrete, depending on how the generalization is stated. The superclass in Figure 5.1 is concrete, because only some subclasses are shown. Other
Product possibilities (such as clothes, movies, and pet supplies) lack a corresponding subclass.

Figure 5.2 reworks the generalization, adding an *OtherProduct* subclass, and makes the
generalization complete. With the revised model, every superclass occurrence is covered by
one of the subclasses. Therefore the *Product* class in Figure 5.2 is abstract.

As a matter of style, it is a good idea to avoid concrete superclasses. Then, abstract and
concrete classes are readily apparent at a glance; all superclasses are abstract and all leaf subclasses are concrete.

Exercise 5.7 addresses the distinction between abstract and concrete superclasses.

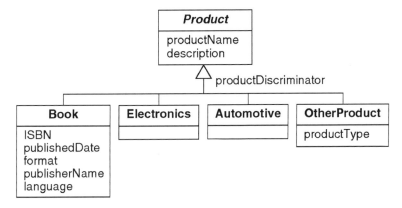

Figure 5.2 Avoiding concrete superclasses with the UML. You can always eliminate concrete superclasses by introducing an *Other* subclass.

5.3 IE Notation

Table 5.1 shows corresponding UML and IE terminology. Figure 5.3 restates Figure 5.2 using IE. IE subtypes are dependent entity types because each subtype primary key refers to the supertype primary key. For example, *Book.bookID* refers to *Product.productID*. The supertype may be independent or dependent (but is usually independent) based on whether its primary key incorporates a foreign key from another entity type.

UML Concept	IE Concept
Generalization	Subtyping
Superclass	Supertype
Subclass	Subtype
Generalization set name	Discriminator

Table 5.1 Corresponding terminology for generalization

With IE, all subtyping is complete and the supertype is always abstract. However, IE does have two kinds of subtyping. With *exclusive* subtyping, the subtypes are disjoint and each supertype occurrence has one subtype occurrence. With *inclusive* subtyping, subtypes can overlap and each supertype occurrence can have multiple subtype occurrences. As Figure 5.3 shows, the IE notation for exclusive subtyping is a semicircle enclosing an 'X'. Chapter 8 discusses inclusive subtyping. The vast majority of models use only exclusive subtyping. Inclusive subtyping seldom occurs.

Exercises 5.8 and 5.9 address IE notation for generalization.

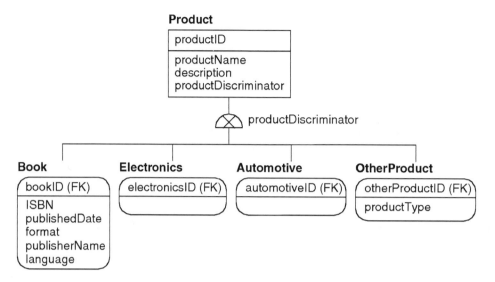

Figure 5.3 IE notation for generalization. The vast majority of
models use only exclusive subtyping.

5.4 Multiple Generalization Levels

There can be multiple generalization levels. An occurrence of a subclass is simultaneously
an occurrence of all its superclasses. A subclass in one generalization may be a superclass in
another. Figure 5.4 extends the *Product* hierarchy for the online retail example (with only
some attributes shown). Figure 5.5 shows the same hierarchy with the IE notation. In practice, there are many more classes than the excerpt shows.

With generalization the description is fragmented but the object itself accumulates detail
(attributes, operations, and associations) from each generalization level. Thus, *Laptop* adds
data from *Product*, *Electronics*, and *Computer* to its own direct data

Note that the IE model renames the inherited keys. Our practice is to make each ID name
match the entity type name. Thus *Book* renames *productID* to *bookID*, *Computer* renames
electronicsID to *computerID*, and so forth. If you don't do this renaming, associations to the
various levels can become ambiguous and confusing. Exercise 5.9 illustrates this point.

We recommend that you simplify deeply nested generalizations because they can be difficult to understand. As a guideline, generalization should have no more than five levels.

Exercise 5.6 can help you check your understanding of multiple generalization levels.

5.5 Practical Tips

Consider the following practical tips:

- **Use of generalization**. Do consider adding generalization to deepen the structure of your
  models. However, make sure you only use generalization where a similarity and difference organization truly applies. As a rough guideline, most database models should have
  no more than a few generalizations per each hundred classes.

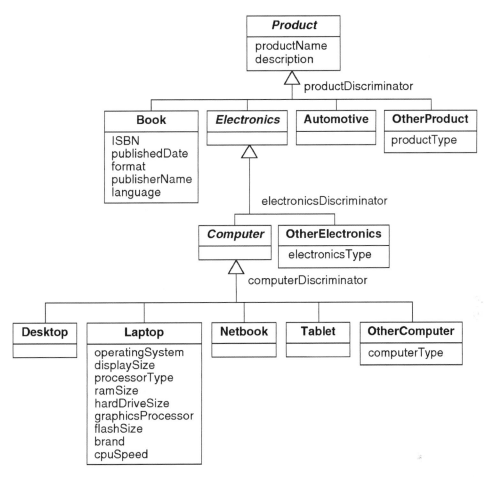

Figure 5.4 Multi-level generalization hierarchy with the UML notation.
A subclass inherits the data of its superclasses.

- **Concrete superclasses**. Avoid concrete superclasses. Then, abstract and concrete classes are apparent at a glance—all superclasses are abstract and all leaf subclasses are concrete. You can always eliminate a concrete superclass by introducing an *Other* subclass.

- **Deeply nested generalizations**. Try to avoid generalizations with more than five levels.

5.6 Chapter Summary

Generalization couples a class (the superclass) to one or more variations of the class (the subclasses). Generalization organizes classes by their similarities and differences, structuring the description of objects. The superclass holds common data; the subclasses add specific data.

An abstract class has no direct occurrences. A concrete class may have direct occurrences. As a matter of style, it is a good idea to avoid concrete superclasses. You can always eliminate a concrete superclass by introducing an *Other* subclass.

Table 5.2 summarizes generalization concepts.

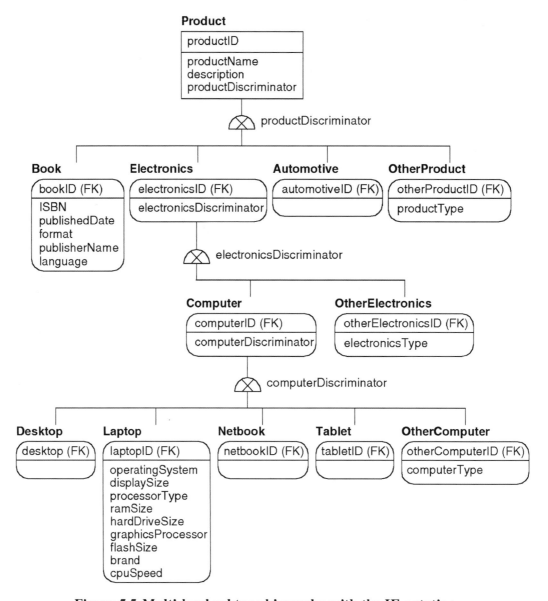

Figure 5.5 Multi-level subtype hierarchy with the IE notation

Exercises

Each exercise has a difficulty level ranging from 1 (easy) to 10 (very difficult).

5.1   (4) For the baseball problem, does it make any sense to combine *PlayerAssignment* with *UmpireAssignment*? Start with the answer to Exercise 4.1.

5.2   (3) Extend the spa model from Exercise 4.3 by adding a generalization for different kinds of payments (credit cards, debit cards, cash, gift certificates).

UML Concept	UML Notation	IE Concept	IE Notation	Definition
Generalization		Subtyping		An organization of classes by their similarities and differences, structuring the description of objects.
Superclass		Supertype		The common attributes, operations, and associations for a generalization.
Subclass		Subtype		Specific attributes, operations, and associations for a generalization.
Generalization set name		Discriminator		An enumerated attribute that indicates the subclass that applies for each superclass occurrence.
Abstract class				A class with no direct occurrences.
Concrete class				A class that can have direct occurrences.

Table 5.2 Terminology summary

5.3 (8) Figure E5.1 shows a model for food products. A *FoodProduct* has multiple *Ingredients*, multiple *NutritionFacts*, and possible *Allergens* listed. For example, the Promax energy bar is made from protein blend, soy protein crisps, casein, and other ingredients. The wrapper lists nutrition facts (amounts) for various nutrition descriptors (total fat, cholesterol, sodium, and protein). There is also a warning for customers allergic to milk and nuts.

   The model has a flaw — a *FoodProduct* may not only contain *Ingredients* but it may also contain lesser *FoodProducts*. Use generalization to improve the model.

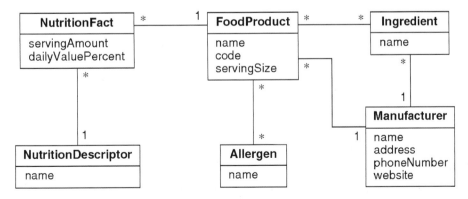

Figure E5.1 Initial model for food products

5.4   (6) Here are classes for a checking account model — Bank, Check, CheckingAccount, Customer, Debit, Deposit, Fee, Interest, Statement, Transaction, Transfer.

Here are attributes — accountNumber, address, amount, checkNumber, currentBalance, description, feeType, name, phone, postingDate, referenceNumber, statementBeginDate, statementBeginBalance, statementEndDate, statementEndBalance.

Construct a UML model with one generalization. Add associations as appropriate. You should represent *Transaction* as a superclass; some of the listed classes are subclasses. Assign attributes to the proper class(es).

5.5   (4) Use generalization to restructure and simplify the model in Figure E5.2. The model describes a security database that records all password-related activity for an *Account*.

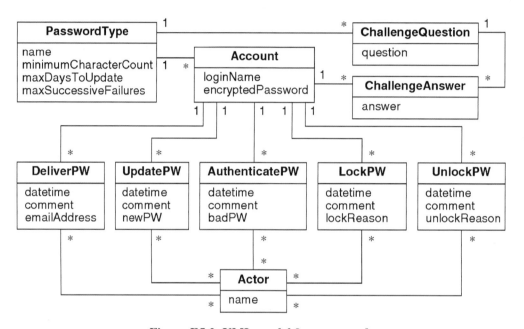

Figure E5.2 UML model for passwords

An *Account* provides the means for a user to access computing resources. Each *Account* has a unique *loginName* and *encryptedPassword* value. The model tracks various password actions that can occur for an *Account*. An *Actor* is a person involved in password actions such as a user, service representative, or administrator.

Each *Account* has a *PasswordType* that dictates the possible *ChallengeQuestions* that are asked if the user forgets the *Account* password. When an *Account* is set up, the user provides *ChallengeAnswers* to some of the *ChallengeQuestions*.

DeliverPW delivers the password for an *Account* to the user. *UpdatePW* may go through one or more challenge questions as part of changing an account's password. *AuthenticatePW* determines if the user attempt to access an *Account* has provided a correct password and logs the *badPW* otherwise. Examples of *lockReason* include excessive failure attempts, customer request, and system detection of suspicious activity. Examples of *unlockReason* include service rep decision and system error correction.

5.6   (5) Consider an application for managing syndicated loans. The loans can be huge, involving billions of dollars, and can arise from lending to governments and multinational corporations. Participation in a loan must be spread across multiple lenders because the risk is too large for a single lender.

An *Asset* is something of value and can be a *Currency* (such as US Dollars, Euros, and Yen), a *LoanInstrument*, or an *OtherAsset* (such as bonds and stocks).

A *LoanInstrument* can be a *FacilityAgreement*, *Tranche*, or *TrancheItem*. A *FacilityAgreement* is an overall financial amount that is available to a borrower. A *Tranche* is a loan that is made under the auspices of a *FacilityAgreement*. A *TrancheItem* is the portion of a *Tranche* covered by a particular lender. Thus a *Tranche* splits into *TrancheItems*, one for each lender.

Prepare a UML generalization hierarchy for these requirements. Just show classes and omit attributes.

5.7 (3) Consider the superclasses in your answer to the prior exercise. Note whether each one is concrete or abstract.

5.8 (2) Convert this book's answer for Exercise 5.6 to an IE diagram.

5.9 (5) Restate the IE diagram for this book's answer to Exercise 5.8 so that subtypes do not rename foreign key references to the supertype. Note the confusion between foreign keys for relationship types and foreign keys for generalizations.

Test 1

Basic Modeling Concepts

1. Consider the following analogies. Class is to object as:
   a. Association is to link
   b. Attribute is to value
   c. Both (a) and (b)
   d. Neither (a) nor (b)

2. Is it possible to define a separate domain for each attribute in a data model? Explain your answer.
   a. Yes
   b. No

3. Consider the models in Figure T1.1. Both are correct models. Which is the better model?
   a. Top model
   b. Bottom model

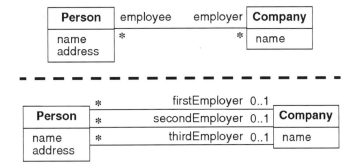

Figure T1.1 UML models for employment

4. Consider the models in Figure T1.2. Both are correct models. Which is the better model?
   a. Left model
   b. Right model

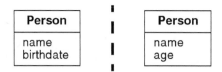

Figure T1.2 UML models for person

5. Is the data in Figure T1.3 consistent with the model in Figure 2.1? Explain your answer.
    a. Yes
    b. No

Hello John Doe.

Your order was sent to
John Doe
123 Main Street
New York, New York 10453 USA

Shipment details:
Prague Winter: A Personal Story of Remembrance and War — $17.99
Shipping and Handling — $3.99
Total cost — $21.98

Figure T1.3 Data for a sample order from a Web site

6. Is Figure T1.4 a valid UML model? Explain your answer.
    a. Yes
    b. No

A	c1		B
a1 a2 a3	1 1 c2	* *	b1 b2 b3 b4

Figure T1.4 UML model that may or may not be valid

7. Is Figure T1.5 a valid IE model? Explain your answer.
    a. Yes
    b. No

8. Is Figure T1.6 a valid UML model? Explain your answer.
    a. Yes
    b. No

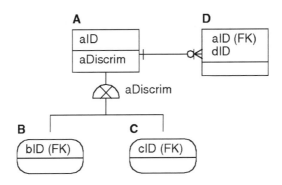

Figure T1.5 IE model that may or may not be valid

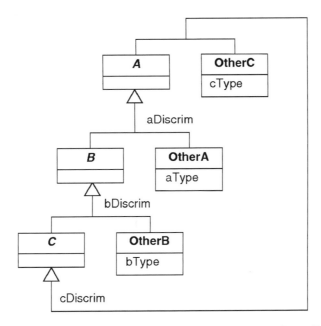

Figure T1.6 UML model that may or may not be valid

9. Do the models in Figure T1.7 describe the same occurrences? Explain your answer.
    a. Yes
    b. No

10. Suppose you are building software to manage a reporting hierarchy. Which model in Figure T1.8 is better? Explain your answer.
    a. Left model
    b. Right model

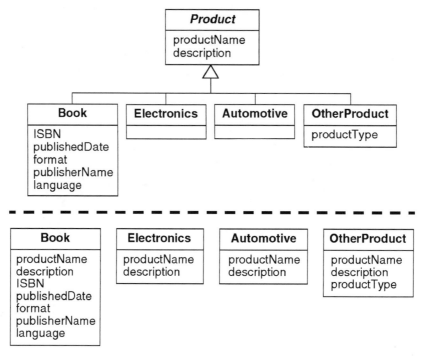

Figure T1.7 UML models for product

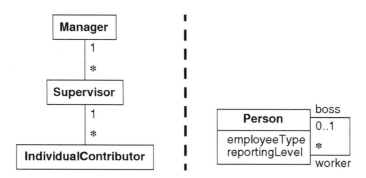

Figure T1.8 UML models for a management reporting hierarchy

Part 2

Advanced Modeling Concepts

Part 2 builds on Part 1 and covers advanced modeling concepts. You will need these concepts to construct UML data models for large and complex problems.

Chapter 6 presents advanced class concepts, starting with a discussion of identity. With existence-based identity, a system-generated attribute (called a surrogate key) identifies objects. With value-based identity, a unique combination of real-world attributes (called a natural key) identifies objects. I normally use existence-based identity for my applications. The next topic is derived data — data that can be determined from other data. You should use derived data sparingly, as it adds bulk and complicates development. The chapter concludes with a discussion of current data vs. historical data.

Chapter 7 covers advanced association concepts. An association class is an association that is also a class. Like the links of an association, the occurrences of an association class derive identity from the related objects. Like a class, an association class can have attributes, operations, and associations. An ordered association imposes a physical ordering on the objects of a "many" association end. A qualified association is an association in which a qualifier attribute distinguishes among the objects for a "many" association end.

Chapter 8 explains multiple inheritance, in which the inheritance structure forms a directed graph; this is more complex than the single inheritance trees in Chapter 5. One form of multiple inheritance is multiple generalization in which a subclass inherits from more than one generalization. Another form is overlapping generalization in which a superclass occurrence can have multiple subclass occurrences for the same generalization. The chapter finishes with a discussion of large taxonomies and a comparison of generalization to other modeling constructs.

Chapter 9 explains techniques for presenting large models that do not readily fit on a single piece of paper.

How do you tell if a model is any good? Chapter 10 describes several different ways for assessing data model quality. Normal forms are a classical part of database theory and data models should observe them, unless there are compelling reasons otherwise. (Data warehouse models typically violate normal forms for compelling reasons.) A sound model should also take advantage of non-structural constraints that a database can enforce. Robert Hillard takes a different approach and likens a data model to a graph; he uses graph metrics to assess model complexity. Steve Hoberman has devised a scorecard for measuring model quality.

The self-assessment test can help you judge your comprehension of Part 2.

6

Advanced Class Concepts

This chapter discusses additional aspects of classes and builds on the basic concepts from Chapter 3. We cover database keys, derived data, and historical data.

6.1 Candidate, Primary, and Alternate Keys

As Figure 6.1 shows, the UML and IE differ in their treatment of keys. The UML *Customer* class corresponds to two different IE models. The left IE model specifies *customerID* (a generated unique number) as the primary key. The right IE model uses *loginName* as the primary key and foregoes *customerID*. Before proceeding, let us define some terminology.

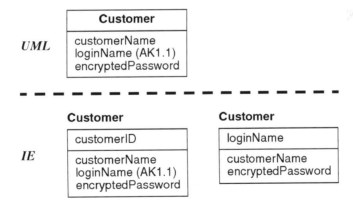

Figure 6.1 Alternative models. An IE model makes decisions about identity that a UML model defers.

A *candidate key* is a combination of one or more attributes that uniquely identifies each record within a table. The attributes in a candidate key must be minimal; that means no attribute can be discarded without destroying uniqueness. No attribute in a candidate key can be null. An attribute may participate in multiple candidate keys. Database software can efficiently enforce the uniqueness of candidate keys, so it is important to specify them.

A *primary key* is an arbitrary choice of candidate key that is used for foreign key references. A table can have at most one primary key and normally should have one. The UML
notation assumes that each class has an implicit identifier that is the primary key. IE explicitly
lists primary key attributes in the top portion of the entity type box.

Note that the choice of primary keys is an artifact. The UML properly defers these decisions until later in development. IE forces premature attention to primary keys, detracting
from focus on the business problem and choices of representation. During early modeling,
the emphasis should be on a model's structure and scope — the UML does this well. As development proceeds to physical design, it is helpful to show primary keys and their propaga-
tion (this is needed to build the database) — IE does this well.

An *alternate key* is a candidate key that is not chosen as a primary key. Therefore each
candidate key is either a primary key or an alternate key. A table can have any number of alternate keys. IE uses the notation *AKn.m* to indicate the mth attribute for the nth alternate key.
The UML has no specified notation for unique keys, so we will also use the *AKn.m* notation
for UML models.

Exercises 6.1 and 6.4 can help you check your understanding of keys.

6.2 Surrogate Key vs. Natural Key

Figure 6.2 shows an excerpt of the online retail model from Chapter 2. Figure 6.3 and Figure
6.4 show two IE approaches to defining primary keys — existence-based identity and mostly
value-based identity.

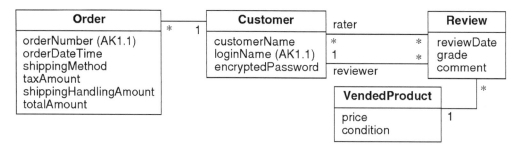

Figure 6.2 Excerpt of UML model for online retail

With *existence-based identity* (Figure 6.3) each class has a generated identifier (also called
a *surrogate key*) as its primary key. Each association has a primary key composed of identifiers from the related classes. The advantage of this approach is that each class's primary key
is a single attribute (often defined as a number). Furthermore, since the primary key is synthetic, it is immutable (not subject to change) — so there is no need to propagate updates to
foreign key references. The use of existence-based identity presumes convenient access to an
ID generator (such as Oracle sequence numbers and the SQL Server identity data type).
Unique combinations of real-world attributes can still (and should) be enforced — that is the
purpose of alternate keys.

Another approach is *value-based identity* — a unique combination of real-world attributes
(also called a *natural key*) identifies each class occurrence. "Real-world attributes" are those

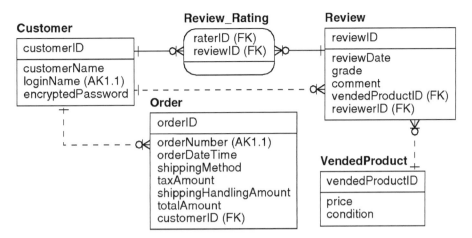

Figure 6.3 An IE model (with existence-based identity)

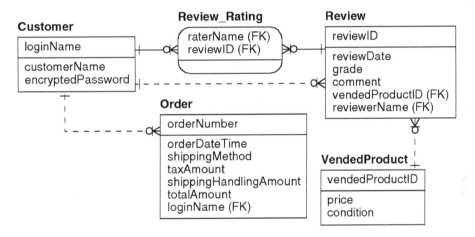

Figure 6.4 Another IE model (with mostly value-based identity)

that come from the business problem description. Figure 6.4 mixes existence-based identity and value-based identity. *Customer* and *Order* have value-based identity. The advantage is that primary keys have intrinsic meaning. A downside is that the value of real-world attributes can change — such changes must propagate to foreign keys. Also, some objects (such as *Review*) lack value-based identifiers. Some models have a series of dependent entity types that lead to unwieldy multi-attribute primary keys. (See Exercise 7.11 in the next chapter.)

Exercises 6.2 and 6.3 illustrate the distinction between existence-based and value-based identity.

6.3 Derived Data

Derived data is data that can be computed from other data. Classes, attributes, and associations can all be derived. In Figure 6.5, a person's age can be computed from the birthdate and

Figure 6.5 Derived attribute. Derived data is data that can be computed from other data.

the current date. The UML notation for derived data is to precede the name with a slash. IE has no specific notation for derived data, but you can add a comment on the diagram.

As a general rule, you should use derived data sparingly — derived data adds bulk to a model and seldom adds clarity. Furthermore, derived data complicates development, as it can be difficult to keep derived data consistent with its base data. For example, if the *Person* table had an age column, the table would need to be updated daily for the persons whose birthday is that day.

Figure 6.6 shows another example. There is no good reason to add a derived association from *OrderItem* to *Product*, as this information can be readily (and efficiently) obtained by traversing from *OrderItem* to *VendedProduct* to *Product*.

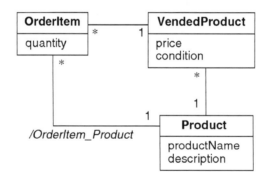

Figure 6.6 A derived association. Use derived data sparingly because it complicates development and seldom improves performance.

6.4 Current vs. Historical Data

The business requirements determine if historical data is important. Looking at the order model in Chapter 2, there are several attributes that deal with time: *Orders.orderDateTime*, *Book.publishedDate*, and *Review.reviewDate*. For other portions of the model, time is clearly unimportant — the list of *Authors* for a *Book* is fixed and does not change. A more robust model would need to address several questions:

- Should there be a history of *Addresses* for a *Customer* with effective and expiration dates? Figure 6.7 shows models for current and historical address data.

- Is it important to keep a history of when *Products* and *VendedProducts* go on and off the market?

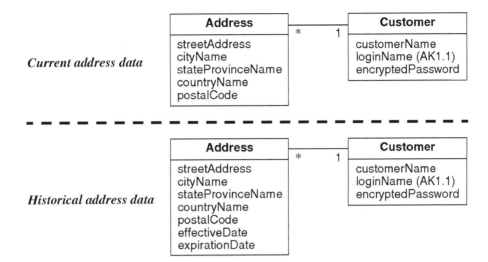

Figure 6.7 Current vs. historical data. Business requirements determine if there is a need for historical data.

- Is it important to track changes in the *price* of a *VendedProduct*? Then it would be helpful to keep a price history.

Exercises 6.5 through 6.8 can help you verify your understanding of historical data.

6.5 Modeling Pitfalls

You should look out for the following pitfalls:

- **Reconsider large classes**. Be suspicious of classes with twenty attributes or more. Some of these classes may be reasonable and just have much descriptive data. Other classes may lack cohesion and have a jumble of data. Also be wary of classes that are difficult to define. You should restructure these disjointed classes into more fundamental classes.

- **Avoid parallel attributes**. Normally, avoid groups of similar attributes. (Data warehouses can violate this rule.) Such parallel attributes often codify arbitrary decisions and reduce flexibility. In Figure 6.8 there is nothing special about estimate, re-estimate, and actual — these are just three possible values for *CostBasis*. Similarly, material, labor, and tax are three possibilities for *CostItem*. Widespread use of parallel attributes can indicate a poorly conceived model.

- **Avoid anonymous attributes**. Clearly describe the data being stored. With the left model of Figure 6.9 it is not clear which attribute has city name. Furthermore, the attribute with city name might vary by record. As an exception, it is acceptable to have a small number of user-defined attributes.

- **Do declare data**. A relational database is declarative. Accordingly, you should declare data in your models. Do not use cryptic codes. As Figure 6.10 shows, a database should declare enumerations and not bury them in programming code. Therefore, *paymentType* should either be a meaningful string (top right model) or a code that another table defines (bottom right model).

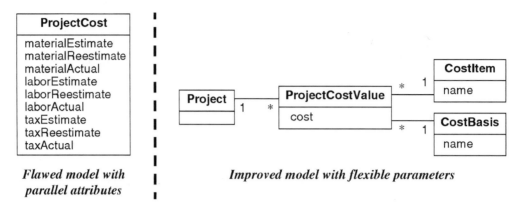

Figure 6.8 Parallel attributes. Normally avoid parallel attributes because they codify arbitrary decisions and reduce flexibility.

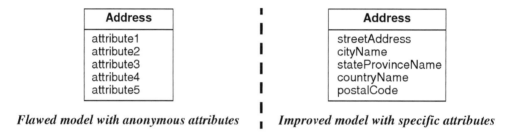

Figure 6.9 Anonymous attributes. Clearly describe the data being stored.

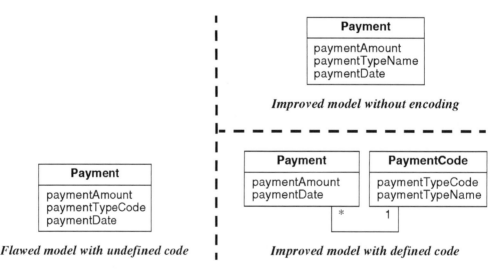

Figure 6.10 Declaring data. Do declare data such as enumerations.

Exercises 6.9 through 6.11 illustrate some of these modeling pitfalls.

6.6 Practical Tips

Consider the following tips as you construct models:

- **Unique keys**. Do define unique combinations of attributes that arise.
- **Synthetic vs. natural keys**. Unless there are unusual circumstances, we recommend the use of surrogate keys (existence-based identity).
- **Lexicon**. Chapter 3 advocated the use of naming standards. In particular, it is helpful to have a naming rule for synthetic keys. This book uses a suffix of 'ID' to indicate synthetic keys.
- **Derived data**. Use derived data sparingly. Note any derived data with the UML slash prefix or an IE comment.
- **History**. Actively consider the trade-offs between current and historical data.
- **Pitfalls**. Step back from your models and make sure that you avoid the pitfalls that we have listed: large classes, parallel attributes, anonymous attributes, and missing data declaration.

6.7 Chapter Summary

There are two approaches to identity in a data model. With existence-based identity, a system-generated attribute (also called a surrogate key) identifies objects. With value-based identity, a unique combination of real-world attributes (also called a natural key) identifies objects. We recommend existence-based identity because there are advantages and little downside.

Derived data is data that can be determined from other data. You should use derived data sparingly, as it adds bulk and can complicate development. Note all derived data with the UML slash notation or an IE comment.

Often, when constructing a model, you have a choice of capturing current data only or including historical data as well. The business requirements ultimately determine the appropriate choice.

Table 6.1 summarizes UML and IE concepts.

UML Concept	IE Concept	Definition
	Candidate key	A combination of one or more attributes that uniquely identifies each record within a table. The attributes in a candidate key must be minimal. No attribute in a candidate key can be null.
	Primary key	A candidate key that is chosen for foreign key references.
	Alternate key	A candidate key that is not chosen as a primary key.
Object identifier	Surrogate key	A system-generated attribute that identifies each object.
	Natural key	A unique combination of real-world attributes that identifies each object.
Derived data		Data that can be determined from other data.

Table 6.1 Terminology summary

Bibliographic Notes

[Khoshafian-1986] is a classic reference that explains identity for programming languages and databases. [Blaha-2010] and [Fowler-1997] also discuss subtle aspects of identity.

[Song-2004] presents an approach to constructing class models from requirements and unifies multiple approaches in the literature.

References

[Blaha-2010] Michael Blaha. *Patterns of Data Modeling*. New York: CRC Press, 2010.

[Fowler-1997] Martin Fowler. *Analysis Patterns: Reusable Object Models*. Boston: Addison-Wesley, 1997.

[Khoshafian-1986] SN Khoshafian and GP Copeland. Object identity. *OOPSLA '86 as ACM SIG-PLAN 21*, 11 (November 1986), 406–416.

[Song-2004] Il-Yeol Song, Kurt Yano, Juan Trujillo, and Sergio Lujan-Mora. A taxonomic class modeling methodology for object-oriented analysis. *Information Modeling Methods and Methodologies*, 2004, 216–240.

Exercises

Each exercise has a difficulty level ranging from 1 (easy) to 10 (very difficult).

6.1 (3) Add alternate keys to the answer for Exercise 3.6.

6.2 (3) Prepare an IE model for the answer to Exercise 6.1, using existence-based identity.

6.3 (3) Prepare an IE model for the answer to Exercise 6.1, using value-based identity where possible, and existence-based identity otherwise.

6.4 (7) Elaborating the online auction example from Exercise 4.4, customers are uniquely identified with a *userID* string. We can readily add *userID* as an attribute of the *Customer* class. It is easy for a customer to change his/her *userID*. How do you think an online auction company would have implemented identity for customers in their database? Is *userID* the primary key of *Customer* or is there some other primary key?

6.5 (3) Revise the online retail model from Chapter 2 to keep a history of when *Products* and *VendedProducts* go on and off the market.

6.6 (6) Revise the educational course model from the answer to Exercise 3.7 so that it can track when *Departments* are started and terminated for an *Institution*, as well as when *Teachers* join and leave a *Department*.

6.7 (7) Consider the models in Figure E6.1 for historical address data. What is the difference between the two models?

6.8 (7) Restate the models from Figure E6.1 so that they only store current data.

6.9 (8) Figure E6.2 shows a first attempt at a model for vehicle rental data. After constructing this model, the developer realized that the *Reservation* class was missing and that some of the *VehicleRental* data really pertains to *Reservation*. Revise this model to include a *Reservation* class.

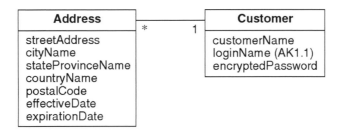

Figure E6.1 Alternative models for historical address data

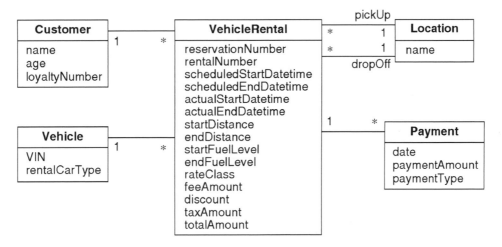

Figure E6.2 First attempt at a model for vehicle rental data

6.10 (5) Figure E6.3 shows a sample driver's license, and Figure E6.4 is a first attempt at a model. (The stick figure is a photo. Please forgive the lack of artistry.) Note that the modeler has placed many attributes into a *DriversLicense* class. Add the following classes to the model (*StateProvince*, *Address*, and *Person*). Add associations and reassign attributes as appropriate.

6.11 (5) For the driver's license model, is it better to name the class *Person* or *Driver*? Discuss the trade-offs.

Missouri Driver License

License Number D0478625
Class F

SANTANA, SALLY AGNES
456 Center Street
Springfield, MO 65807

Birthdate	**Expiration Date**
10-31-1973	10-31-2016

Female   5'06   140 lbs   Brown Eyes
  Restrictions   Endorsements
           Y

Willing to be an organ donor   YES

Signature   -----------------------------------

Figure E6.3 Sample driver's license

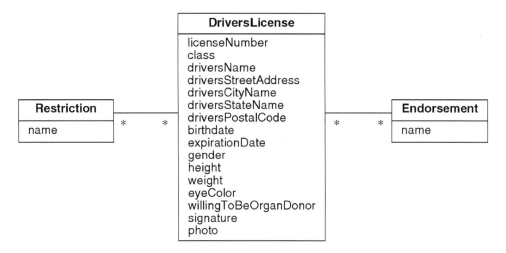

Figure E6.4 First attempt at driver's license model

7

Advanced Association Concepts

This chapter explains associations further and builds on the basic concepts from Chapter 4. We cover association classes, ordered associations, qualified associations and ternary associations. Association classes and qualified associations are notable UML constructs that are not found in most other database notations.

7.1 Association Class

An *association class* is an association that is also a class. Like the links of an association, the occurrences of an association class derive identity from the related objects. Like a class, an association class can have attributes, operations, and associations.

The UML notation for an association class is a box that connects to the corresponding association with a dotted line. Figure 7.1 shows an association class between *Customer* and *Review*. A customer can rate a review and note if it is helpful. As you can see from the IE model, the identity of the association class propagates from *Customer* and *Review*. The combination of a *rater Customer* and a *Review* has the attribute *isHelpful*. An association class may have a name, but the UML does not require it.

Many-to-many associations provide a compelling rationale for association classes. Attributes unmistakably belong to such an association and cannot be ascribed to either class. The *isHelpful* attribute belongs to the combination of a *rater Customer* and a *Review*, not to either one individually.

Figure 7.2 shows a possible extension of review capabilities for the online retail example. A *rater Customer* can also comment. To control dialog, a *StaffMember* approves each comment before it is posted. The model tracks who approved each comment and when it was approved. As Figure 7.2 demonstrates, an association class can have further associations.

The example in Figure 7.3 demonstrates the difference between an ordinary class and an association class. The association class has at most one occurrence for each pairing of *Customer* and *Review*. The ordinary class allows any number of *Review_Ratings* for a *Customer* and *Review*.

Exercises 7.1 through 7.4 can verify your understanding of association classes.

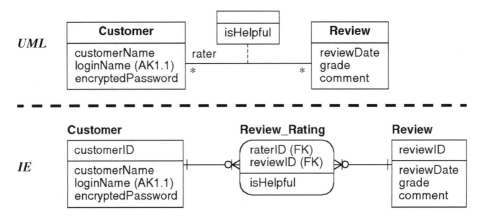

Figure 7.1 Notation for association class. An association class is
an association that is also a class.

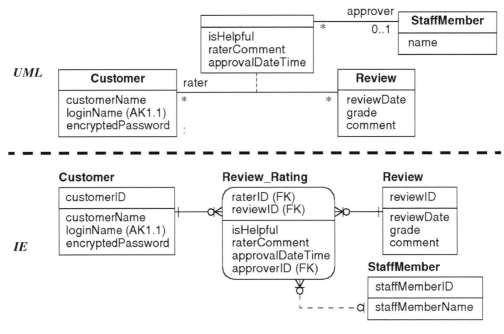

Figure 7.2 UML association class. Like a class, an association class
can have attributes, operations, and associations.

7.2 Ordered Association

By default, the objects for a "many" association end are a set and therefore lack order. Sometimes, however, the objects have an explicit order that you can indicate by writing "{or-
dered}" next to the association end. An *ordered association* imposes sequencing on a "many"
association end.

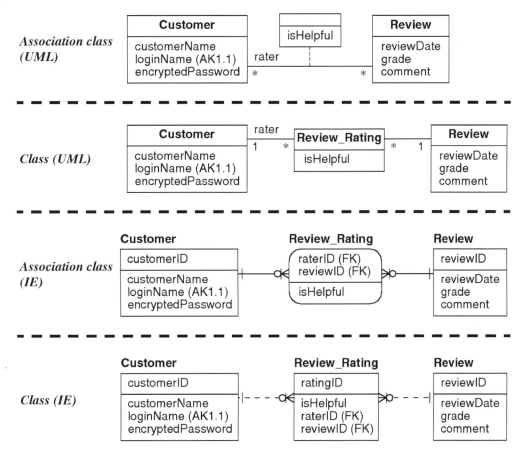

Figure 7.3 Association class vs. ordinary class. An association class has at most one occurrence for each combination of constituent objects.

In Figure 7.4, multiple authors of a book have a listed order. The sequence number in the IE model effects the ordering. In the IE model, the combination of *bookID* and *sequenceNumber* is an alternate key.

You can verify your understanding of ordered associations with Exercise 7.5.

7.3 Qualified Association

A *qualified association* is an association in which a *qualifier* attribute distinguishes among the objects for a "many" association end. Associations that are one-to-many and many-to-many can have qualifiers. The qualifier selects among the target objects, reducing the effective multiplicity, often from "many" to one. Qualified associations with a target multiplicity of one specify a precise path for finding the target object from the source object.

The UML notation is a small box on the association end near the source class. The source class plus the qualifier yields the target class. In Figure 7.5, an *Order* has many *OrderItems*. An *Order* plus an *itemNumber* yields at most one *OrderItem*.

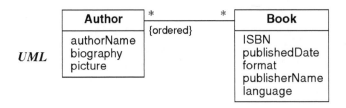

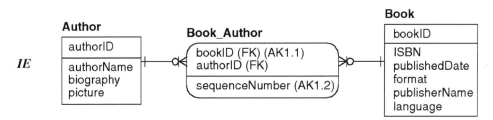

Figure 7.4 Ordered association. The objects for a "many" association
end can have an explicit order

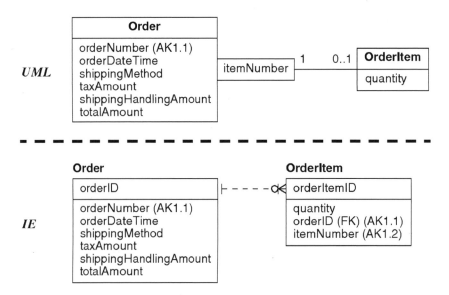

Figure 7.5 Notation for qualified association. A qualified association selects among the
target objects, reducing the effective multiplicity, often from "many" to one.

Figure 7.6 restates the model without the qualifier. Figure 7.6 has exactly the same meaning as Figure 7.5 aside from the omitted qualifier constraint. Both models are correct, but the qualified model adds information (the constraint).

Exercises 7.6 through 7.11 can help you check your understanding of qualified associations.

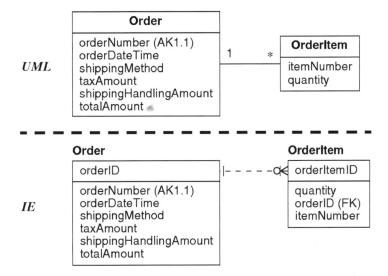

Figure 7.6 Underlying association without the qualifier. A qualified
association adds a constraint to a model.

7.4 Ternary Association

The UML supports ternary and higher order associations, although they seldom occur. A *ternary association* is an association involving three classes. The UML notation is a diamond with lines connecting the related classes. In Figure 7.7, a *ProjectAssignment* is the combination of a *Person* performing a *Task* for a *Project*.

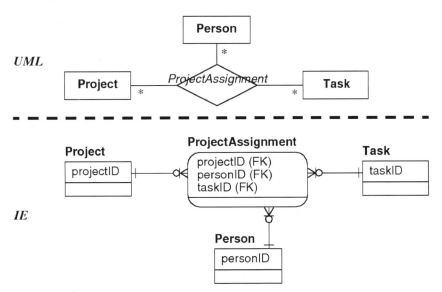

Figure 7.7 Notation for ternary association. A ternary association
involves three classes.

You should avoid ternary and higher order associations. Many supposed "ternary" associations are not fundamental and can be decomposed into binary associations, with possible qualifiers and attributes. *ProjectAssignment* in Figure 7.7 is a true ternary association because it cannot be decomposed without losing information. Each *ProjectAssignment* is uniquely identified by the combination of a *Person*, *Project*, and *Task*. All three classes are needed to identify a *ProjectAssignment*.

For the occasional genuine ternary association, we recommend that you degrade the UML model and promote the association to a class as Figure 7.8 shows. The degraded model loses the constraint that the combination of *Project*, *Person*, and *Task* is unique. The UML comment in curly braces informally adds back the constraint. (IE is more expressive than the UML in this regard, and can structurally capture the uniqueness constraint.) In practice, ternary associations occur so seldom that they are not worth the bother of explaining.

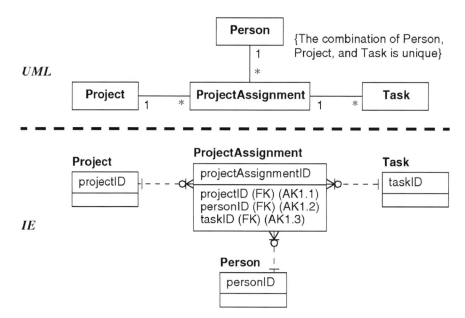

Figure 7.8 Degrading a ternary association. As a practical matter, it is usually best to degrade a genuine ternary association to a class.

7.5 Modeling Pitfalls

You should look out for the following pitfall:

- **Avoid symmetric associations for relational databases**. A symmetric association has the same multiplicity and name on each end. Typically, this is a many-to-many self association. Figure 7.9 shows an example with the resolution (promote a symmetric association to a class). The problem with symmetric associations is that data must be double stored or double searched, as [Blaha-2010] explains.

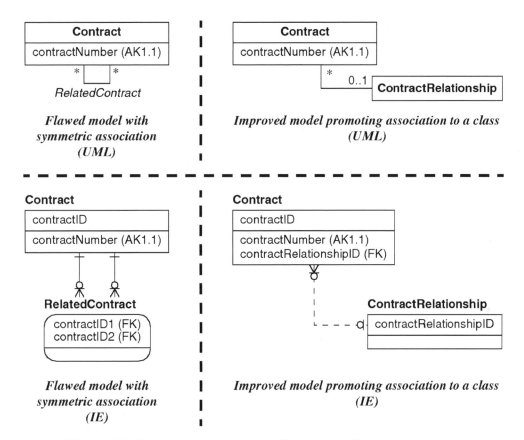

Figure 7.9 Symmetric association. Promote each one to a class.

7.6 Practical Tips

Consider the following tips as you construct models:

- **Association classes**. Note the trade-off between an association class and an ordinary class. An association class enforces the uniqueness of the combination of related classes; an ordinary class has no such constraint. The choice of which to use depends on requirements.

- **Ordered associations**. The UML has notation to express that the objects for a "many" association end have an order.

- **Qualifiers**. Challenge association ends with a multiplicity of "many." Sometimes a qualifier can improve the precision.

- **Ternary associations**. Avoid ternary associations. Many ternary associations can be decomposed into binary associations. If you have a true ternary association, it is usually best to degrade it and restate the ternary as a class.

7.7 Chapter Summary

An association class is an association that is also a class. Like the links of an association, the occurrences of an association class derive identity from the related objects. Like a class, an association class can have attributes, operations, and associations.

Sometimes, the objects on a "many" association end have an explicit order. You can write "{ordered}" next to such an association end.

A qualified association is an association in which a qualifier attribute distinguishes among the objects for a "many" association end. One-to-many and many-to-many associations can have qualifiers. The qualifier selects among the target objects, reducing the effective multiplicity, often from "many" to one. The source class plus the qualifier yields the target class.

The UML supports ternary and higher order associations, even though they seldom occur. A ternary association is an association involving three classes. Many supposed "ternary" associations are not fundamental and can be decomposed into binary associations. For the occasional genuine ternary association, you should degrade the model and promote the association to a class.

Table 7.1 summarizes UML and IE concepts.

UML Concept	IE Concept	Definition
Association class		An association that is also a class. Has dependent identity like an association and detailed data like a class.
Ordered association		A sequencing imposed on a "many" association end.
Qualified association		An association in which a qualifier attribute distinguishes among the objects for a "many" association end.
Ternary association		An association involving three classes.

Table 7.1 Terminology summary

References

[Blaha-2010] Michael Blaha. *Patterns of Data Modeling*. New York: CRC Press, 2010.

Exercises

Each exercise has a difficulty level ranging from 1 (easy) to 10 (very difficult).

7.1   (5) Figure E7.1 shows alternative model excerpts for TV programs from Exercise 4.10. What is the difference in data stored for the two models?

7.2   (3) Construct IE models for Figure E7.1.

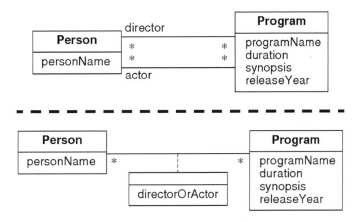

Figure E7.1 Alternative model excerpts for TV programs

7.3 (7) Construct a UML model for the answer to Exercise 3.4. In your model, the price of a *Menu-Item* should be able to vary by *Menu*. Thus the price for a *MenuItem* can vary for breakfast, lunch, or dinner.

7.4 (3) Netflix lets customers rate movies and uses the ratings as a basis for recommendations. Add rating to the answer for Exercise 4.5.

7.5 (6) Consider the answer to the food product exercise from Exercise 5.3. How would you modify the model to indicate that some ingredients are more important than others?

7.6 (6) Figure E7.2 adds a channel qualifier for the TV listing problem from Figure A4.10. The carrier assigns the channel. The channel for a carrier does not lead to a single listing, because the assigned channel can vary by *listingDate* and *startTime*. Which model is better — the original or the revision — and why?

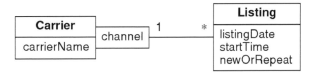

Figure E7.2 Alternative model excerpt for carrier and listing

7.7 (7) Consider the revised model in Figure E7.3. Is Figure E7.3 better or the model in Figure A4.10? Explain your rationale.

Figure E7.3 Another model for carrier and listing

7.8 (3) Construct an IE model for Figure E7.3.

7.9 (7) Revise the course model for the answer to Exercise 3.7 to use qualifiers. Our revision has seven qualifier attributes.

7.10 (5) Revise the checking account problem for the answer to Exercise 5.4 to use qualifiers. Restate *accountNumber* and *statementEndDate* as qualifiers.

7.11 (7) Figure E7.4 shows a UML model. Prepare two different IE models, one with existence-based identity and the other with value-based identity.

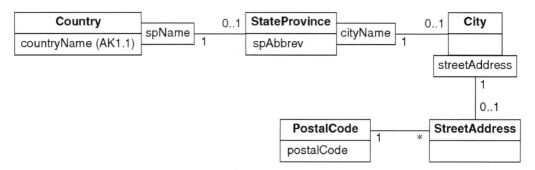

Figure E7.4 Model with a cascade of qualifiers

8

Advanced Generalization Concepts

Chapter 5 explained single inheritance — a generalization where each subclass has one immediate superclass. This chapter covers more complex forms of generalization (multiple inheritance) in which a subclass may have multiple immediate superclasses. It also discusses large taxonomies and compares generalization to other modeling constructs.

8.1 Multiple Inheritance

Multiple inheritance is a mechanism that permits a class to inherit from multiple immediate superclasses. This is a more complex form of generalization than single inheritance, which restricts the class structure to a tree. Multiple inheritance provides greater power in specifying classes, but at the cost of more complexity. There are two motivations for multiple inheritance: model-driven and implementation-driven.

Model-driven multiple inheritance can arise when describing an application. For example an amphibious vehicle is both a land vehicle and a water vehicle. Model-driven multiple inheritance increases conceptual accuracy but complicates a model.

Implementation-driven multiple inheritance can occur when an application mixes functionality from different sources. For example, the application itself may have single inheritance. Multiple inheritance could then arise from mixing in an architectural service from a software library, such as data persistence, auditing, or approval. Implementation-driven multiple inheritance offers the promise of reuse, from blending library code with application code. Once again the downside is added complexity.

8.2 Multiple Generalization

The most common form of multiple inheritance is from separate generalizations. Each subclass inherits from a superclass in each generalization. In Figure 8.1 *OtherMediumVehicle*, *WaterVehicle*, and *LandVehicle* belong to one generalization. *HumanPowerVehicle*, *MotorVehicle*, and *OtherPowerVehicle* belong to another generalization. Each kind of *Vehicle* must specify a medium and propulsion. *Bicycle* is both *LandVehicle* and *HumanPowerVehicle*. The

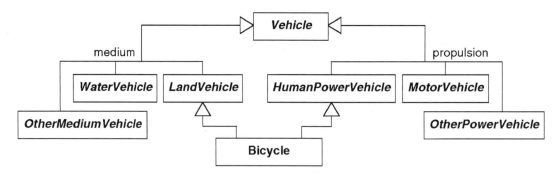

Figure 8.1 Multiple inheritance from disjoint classes. This is the
most common form of multiple inheritance.

model does not show it, but we could define additional combinations, such as motorcycle and
canoe.

A subclass inherits ancestor class data found along multiple paths only once; it is the
same thing. For example, in Figure 8.1 *Bicycle* inherits from *Vehicle* via *medium* and via *propulsion*. However, each *Bicycle* has only a single copy of *Vehicle* data.

Figure 8.2 shows an IE model corresponding to Figure 8.1. IE cannot express that the *ID*
via *LandVehicle* is the same as the *ID* via *HumanPowerVehicle*. Relational databases have
weak support for single generalization (see Chapter 15), so it is not surprising that multiple
generalization is troublesome. Often the best solution is to use a workaround.

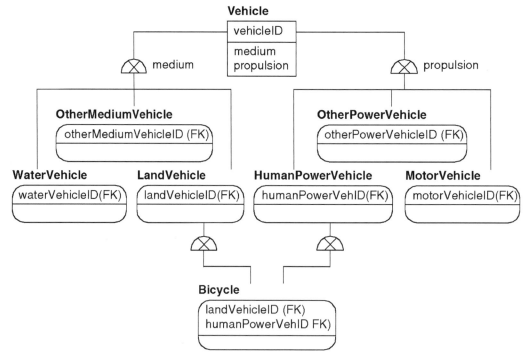

Figure 8.2 IE model with disjoint multiple inheritance. Multiple inheritance is troublesome for relational databases so you will have to use a workaround.

One approach is to degrade generalization to a one-to-one association. The degradation loses the coupling between subclass identity and superclass identity. You can replace all generalizations (Figure 8.3) or all but one generalization (Figure 8.4). These approaches do not require a *Bicycle* class. Rather each bicycle would just be an occurrence of *Vehicle*.

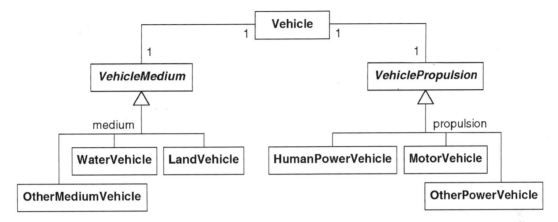

Figure 8.3 Multiple generalization workaround. Replace all generalizations
with one-to-one associations.

Another workaround is to multiply the subtyping bases (Figure 8.5). Factor on one generalization, then on a second, and so forth. For example, three values for *medium* and three values for *propulsion* lead to nine combinations.

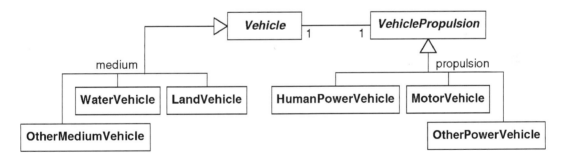

Figure 8.4 Multiple generalization workaround. Replace all but
one generalization with one-to-one associations.

8.3 Overlapping Generalization

Figure 8.6 shows an example of multiple inheritance from overlapping classes. *Amphibious-Vehicle* is both *LandVehicle* and *WaterVehicle*. *LandVehicle* and *WaterVehicle* overlap, because some vehicles travel on both land and water.

Figure 8.7 shows the corresponding IE notation. The lack of an 'X' inside the top semicircle denotes inclusion and possible generalization overlap. The precise meaning of IE inclusive subtyping is not clear.

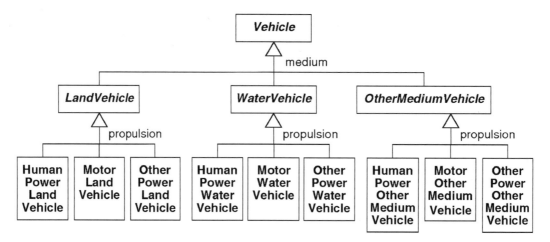

Figure 8.5 Multiple generalization workaround. Multiply the subtyping bases.

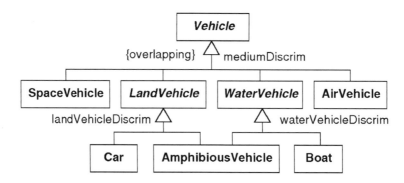

Figure 8.6 Multiple inheritance from overlapping classes. This
kind of multiple inheritance seldom occurs.

We performed an experiment by typing Figure 8.7 into ERwin and defining referential integrity actions. ERwin permits *amphibiousVehicleID* to be defined as a foreign key and refer to both *LandVehicle* and *WaterVehicle*. We generated SQL code (Figure 8.8 shows an excerpt) and ran it with SQL Server. Not surprisingly, the code failed because it does not make sense to have two referents for the same attribute. The SQL Server error message was *Introducing FOREIGN KEY constraint FK4 on table 'WaterVehicle' may cause cycles or multiple cascade paths. Specify ON DELETE NO ACTION or ON UPDATE NO ACTION, or modify other FOREIGN KEY constraints.*

We changed the code for constraints FK3 and FK4 to *no action* and tried it again. The revised script ran successfully with SQL Server. Then we tried inserting some *AmphibiousVehicle* data and it also succeeded. When we tried to delete an *AmphibiousVehicle*, we got another error complaining about referential integrity actions. The intent of these experiments is not to pick on ERwin or SQL Server. Rather, the experiments illustrate the uncertain meaning of multiple inheritance from overlapping classes (which is the same as IE inclusive subtyping.) The fundamental problem is that relational databases do not have a good way of

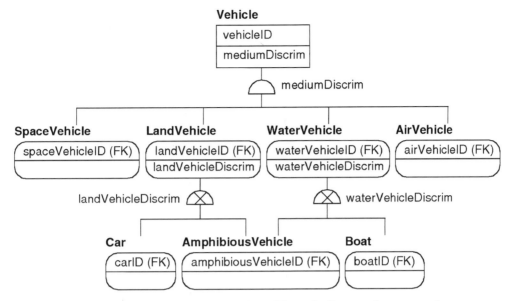

Figure 8.7 IE inclusive subtyping. IE can indicate subtype overlap.

```
CREATE TABLE Vehicle (
    vehicleID        int identity(1,1) NOT NULL ,
    mediaDiscrim     char(18)  NULL ,
    CONSTRAINT PK1 PRIMARY KEY (vehicleID ASC) )
CREATE TABLE LandVehicle (
    landVehicleID   int NOT NULL ,
    CONSTRAINT PK2 PRIMARY KEY (landVehicleID ASC) )
CREATE TABLE WaterVehicle (
    waterVehicleID  int NOT NULL ,
    CONSTRAINT PK3 PRIMARY KEY (waterVehicleID ASC) )
CREATE TABLE AmphibiousVehicle (
    amphibiousVehicleID int NOT NULL ,
    CONSTRAINT PK4 PRIMARY KEY (amphibiousVehicleID ASC) )
ALTER TABLE LandVehicle
    ADD CONSTRAINT FK1 FOREIGN KEY (landVehicleID)
    REFERENCES Vehicle(vehicleID) ON DELETE CASCADE
ALTER TABLE WaterVehicle
    ADD CONSTRAINT FK2 FOREIGN KEY (waterVehicleID)
    REFERENCES Vehicle(vehicleID) ON DELETE CASCADE
ALTER TABLE AmphibiousVehicle
    ADD CONSTRAINT FK3 FOREIGN KEY (amphibiousVehicleID)
    REFERENCES LandVehicle(landVehicleID) ON DELETE CASCADE
ALTER TABLE AmphibiousVehicle
    ADD CONSTRAINT FK4 FOREIGN KEY (amphibiousVehicleID)
    REFERENCES WaterVehicle(waterVehicleID) ON DELETE CASCADE
```

Figure 8.8 ERwin generated code for overlapping generalization.
This code is incorrect and causes a SQL Server error.

implementing overlapping classes, regardless of whether you are using the UML, IE, or some other data modeling notation.

We recommend that you avoid overlapping generalization. In practice, this is not much of a restriction, since it seldom occurs. You can easily restructure a model to eliminate overlapping generalization, as Figure 8.9 shows.

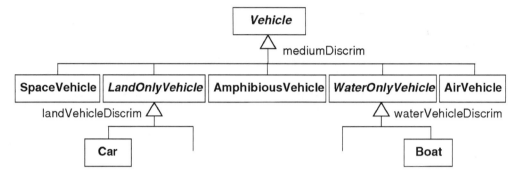

Figure 8.9 Avoiding overlapping generalization. Often the best solution is to rework a model.

8.4 Large Taxonomies

Figure 5.4 shows a partial product hierarchy for the online retail example. You can envision a more complete hierarchy by browsing retail Web sites. The large size of the hierarchy leads to several problems:

- **Devising a hierarchy**. It is difficult to fully comprehend a wide variety of products and fit them into a hierarchy. For example, the categories *Appliances* and *Crafts* could have multiple subcategories and sub-subcategories.

- **Dealing with multiple inheritance**. Some products could appear in multiple places. For example, *Shoes* could be a top-level category and also a subcategory under *Baby Products*. This leads to multiple inheritance in the corresponding model. Previous sections of this chapter discussed the drawbacks of multiple inheritance.

- **Coping with instability**. A large hierarchy involves decisions about where to place each product. Some decisions are clear and likely to be stable. Others are difficult to determine, making the hierarchy tentative and subject to revision.

- **Managing effort**. A large taxonomy leads to many database tables. More tables mean more development effort. The modeler must consider whether a large taxonomy is worth the development cost.

We try to avoid large models because they involve more work. As a guideline, we limit a model to no more than 100 classes. As Figure 8.10 illustrates, abstraction can be used to reduce the size of the online retail product model and increase its flexibility. Figure 8.10 also changes the definition of a hierarchy from a compile-time decision that is difficult to change to a run-time decision that is more flexible.

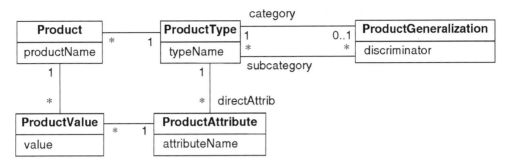

Figure 8.10   Dealing with large taxonomies. Abstraction can reduce the size of a taxonomy and increase its flexibility.

Financial applications can have large taxonomies. Financial concepts include common stocks, preferred stocks, bonds, loans, put options, call options, futures, currencies, and precious metals. Equipment applications can also involve large taxonomies. Equipment concepts include pumps, tanks, motors, mixers, trucks, controllers, excavators, compactors, forklifts, and cranes.

8.5 Analogies

To sharpen the meaning, we compare generalization with other modeling constructs.

8.5.1 Generalization vs. Association

Figure 8.11 compares generalization and association. They both involve two or more classes. The difference is that association describes how two or more objects relate; generalization describes different aspects of a single object.

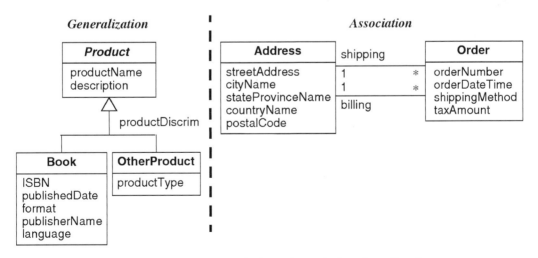

Figure 8.11   Generalization vs. association. Association describes how two or more objects relate; generalization describes different aspects of a single object.

8.5.2 Generalization vs. Instantiation

Generalization relates classes. The superclass describes common data. The subclasses describe specific data. Generalization combines the superclass with subclasses to structure the description of objects.

Instantiation couples an individual object to its defining class. Note that generalization does not deal with individual objects. Therefore, it is incorrect for a generalization to have an individual object as a subclass. In Figure 8.11 it is correct to have *Book* (a class) as a subclass of *Product*. It would be incorrect to have the book "Grapes of Wrath" (an object) as a subclass of *Product*.

8.5.3 Generalization vs. Association End

A subclass is a specialization of a class. An association end is a usage of a class. The subclasses in a generalization partition the superclass's objects. Therefore a subclass involves only some superclass occurrences. There is no such constraint with an association end; an association end may refer to any or all occurrences.

8.5.4 Generalization vs. Enumeration

An enumeration is a listing of permitted values for a domain. A generalization is an organization of classes. The values of a generalization set name (an enumeration) correspond to the subclasses of a generalization. Do not define a generalization to enforce the values of an enumeration.

8.6 Practical Tips

Consider the following tips as you construct models:

- **Forego multiple inheritance**. Avoid multiple inheritance for database applications. Multiple inheritance is difficult to explain and it complicates development. Instead degrade the multiple inheritance or restate the model.

- **Avoid large generalization taxonomies**. Restate a model, if necessary, to avoid a large hierarchy. Consider raising the level of abstraction.

- **Ensure that generalization involves only classes**. It is incorrect for a generalization to have an object as a subclass.

- **Do not define a generalization merely to specify an enumeration**. Generalization relates classes, not values.

8.7 Chapter Summary

Multiple inheritance permits a class to inherit from multiple immediate superclasses. The most common form of multiple inheritance is from separate generalizations. A subclass inherits from a class in each generalization. Multiple inheritance also occurs (infrequently) with overlapping classes.

Multiple generalization is difficult to implement with a relational database. Often the best solution is to use a workaround. One approach is to degrade a generalization to one-to-one associations. Another technique is to multiply the subtyping bases.

Large generalization taxonomies can lead to problems. The very size of a large hierarchy can make it difficult to complete and rationalize the placement of classes. Also a large taxonomy leads to many database tables, increasing the development effort as well as risk. One way to avoid a large taxonomy is to shift the level of abstraction for a model towards more metadata.

Our final topic was to compare generalization to other modeling constructs. Generalization is much different than association. Generalization structures the description of single objects, while association describes how two or more objects relate. Since generalization involves classes, an object cannot take the place of a subclass in a generalization.

Exercises

Each exercise has a difficulty level ranging from 1 (easy) to 10 (very difficult).

8.1   (7) Consider the TV listing problem from Exercise 4.10. Some programs (such as General Hospital) have a series of episodes. *Listing* refers to an *Episode* if there are episodes; otherwise, *Listing* refers to a *Program*. Figure E8.1 shows three alternative models. Comment on the merits of the models. In the top model, a *Listing* corresponds to one *Program* or one *Episode* (intended as exclusive-or). The middle model generalizes *Program* and *Episode* to *ListingItem*. In the bottom model, all programs have episodes; the degenerate case is one episode for a program.

8.2   (3) Add to the model for the answer to Exercise 4.4. As an online auction participant, you can not only bid on items, but you can also "watch" items. A watched item is shown in a special list so that you can easily track bidding activity and see the status for auction closing. You may add a note to a watched item. Software tracks when an auction has ended for a watched item and the item is no longer active.

8.3   (3) Revise the answer to the previous exercise to generalize *Watch* and *Bid*.

8.4   (7) Create tables and populate them for the metamodel in Figure 8.10 with the taxonomy in Figure 5.4.

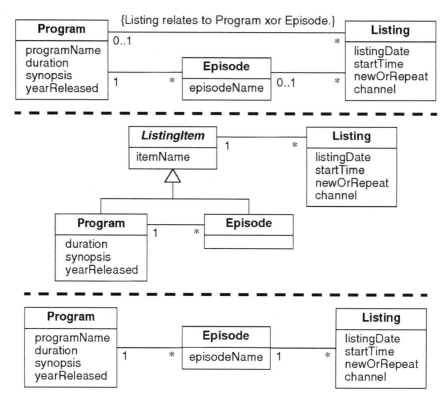

Figure E8.1 Alternative model excerpts for TV programs

9

Packages

A large model cannot readily fit on a single piece of paper. There are two approaches for dealing with large models:

- **One giant diagram**. Developers can present the model as a giant diagram. The diagram is printed on large paper or portions of the diagram are printed on regular paper and taped together.
- **Division into lesser diagrams**. Alternatively, developers can spread a model across multiple diagrams. Each diagram shows part of the model, while an overview diagram ties it all together.

UML packages support the second approach.

9.1 Package

A *package* is a group of elements (classes, associations, generalizations, and lesser packages) with a common theme. The corresponding IE term is *subject area*. Packages add little meaning to a model. Rather they are a convenience for making a model more presentable.

A model consists of one or more packages. Ordinarily, associations and generalizations should appear in a single package. Classes may appear in multiple packages and bind them together. Our convention is to define a class in one package, showing the class name, attributes, and operations. Other packages can reference the class using a class icon annotated with the owner package name, double colon, and then the class name. The class icon does not show any attributes or operations. The UML requires that class and association names be unique within a package. It is a good practice to make these names unique throughout a model.

Developers should place closely related classes in the same package and loosely related classes in different packages. Given this guideline, there are different themes for forming packages. Sometimes there are dominant classes. For example, in Figure 2.1, *Customer* and *Order* are dominant — they connect to much other data. The fundamental purpose of the online retail application is to process orders for customers.

Similarly, a major relationship type can also be the basis for a package. For example, an application model might place a multi-level generalization tree in a single package so the superclasses and subclasses can be seen together.

Major aspects of functionality provide a third basis for forming packages. For example, order functionality and review functionality are much different for the online retail application and would merit separate packages.

And finally, once you have packages in place, take another look at them and see if any packages need to be added to flesh out symmetry.

9.2 Package Example

The online retail model in Figure 2.1 is small enough to fit in a single package. Figure 9.1 through Figure 9.5 show how we might divide the model into multiple packages in preparation for adding detail.

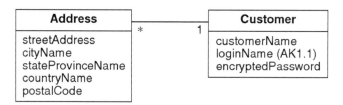

Figure 9.1 Customer package for the online retail application,

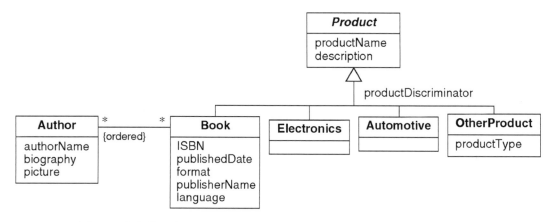

Figure 9.2 Product package for the online retail application.

Figure 9.3 Vended product package for the online retail application.

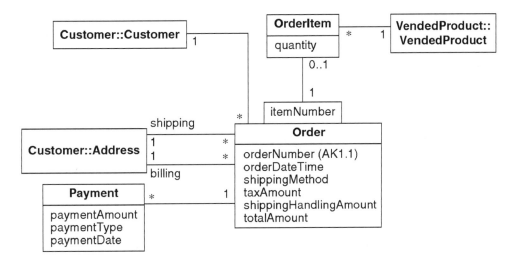

Figure 9.4 Order package for the online retail application.

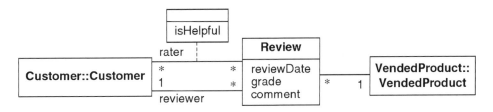

Figure 9.5 Review package for the online retail application.

9.3 Modeling Pitfalls

You should look out for the following pitfalls:

- **Large models**. Generally speaking, you should limit a model to no more than 100 classes. The reason is that large models are more difficult to understand and lead to more development work. Ask yourself if the large size is really justified or whether you can simplify the model. Large models seldom have a compelling justification.

- **Literal modeling**. Your job is not to do what the customer says. Your job is to solve the problem that the customer is imperfectly describing. Accordingly, you must pay attention to the hidden true requirements and interpret and abstract what the customer tells you. Furthermore, you must recognize arbitrary business decisions that could easily change. You can raise abstraction by thinking in terms of patterns.

- **Speculative content**. Do not include content that is not needed now and "might be helpful" in the future. All this does is to make a model larger, increase development time, and raise cost. A model must fully address the requirements, but not greatly exceed them.

9.4 Practical Tips

Consider the following tips as you construct models:

- **Model presentation**. Organize large models into packages so that the reader can understand portions of the model at a time, rather than presenting the whole model all at once.

- **Defining classes**. Define each class in a single package and show its detail there. Other packages that refer to the class should use a class icon, a box that contains the package name, double colon, and the class name (such as *Customer* in Figure 9.5).

- **Diagram layout**. Draw class diagrams in a manner that elicits symmetry. Often there is a superstructure to a problem. Position important classes so that they are visually prominent. Try to avoid crossing lines on diagrams.

- **Model review**. Try to get others to review your models. Expect that your models will require revision. Data models require revision to clarify names, improve abstraction, repair errors, add detail, and tighten structural constraints. Nearly all of our models have required several revisions.

9.5 Chapter Summary

A package is a group of elements (classes, associations, generalizations, and lesser packages) with a common theme. The corresponding IE term is subject area. Packages add little meaning to a model. Rather they are a convenience for making a model more presentable.

A model consists of one or more packages. Ordinarily, associations and generalizations should appear in a single package. Classes may appear in multiple packages and bind them together. You should place closely related classes in the same package and loosely related classes in different packages.

Bibliographic Notes

[Shoval-2004] extends Entity-Relationship modeling so that large diagrams can be expressed as a hierarchy of nested diagrams. They also present a process for creating the hierarchy. Their nesting construct can have relationship types of its own and has deeper meaning than a UML package.

References

[Shoval-2004] Peretz Shoval, Revital Danoch, and Mira Balabam. Hierarchical entity-relationship diagrams: the model, method of creation, and experimental evaluation. *Requirements Engineering*, 2004, 217–228.

Exercises

Each exercise has a difficulty level ranging from 1 (easy) to 10 (very difficult).

9.1   (5) Extend the health spa model from the answer to Exercise 4.3 to support multiple locations.

9.2 (5) Presuming that more detail will be added in the future, how might you organize the model from the answer to Exercise 9.1 into the following packages: *Location*, *Customer*, and *Appointment*. Show models for the three packages.

9.3 (8) Prepare a model of schedules for a sporting league, as well as pricing for seats. Include the following classes and association classes: *ActualPrice*, *BroadcastNetwork*, *Customer*, *Facility*, *Game*, *League*, *ListPrice*, *Season*, *Seat*, *SeatCategory*, and *Team*.

9.4 (5) Presuming that more detail will be added in the future, how might you organize the model from the answer to Exercise 9.3 into two packages. Show models for the two packages.

10

Model Quality

Model quality is important, as models guide database structure. The choice of representations in a model affects the accuracy of stored data, the difficulty of development, and the ability of a database to accommodate change. Model quality can be the difference between the success or failure of an application. This chapter provides several techniques for assessing and improving model quality.

10.1 Normal Forms

A *normal form* is a guideline for relational database design that increases data consistency. There are multiple levels of normal form. Each higher level adds a constraint to the normal form below it. As tables satisfy higher levels of normal forms, they are less likely to store redundant or contradictory data.

A table is in *first normal form* if each row-column combination stores a single value (and not a collection of values). In Figure 10.1a an *OrderItem* can have multiple *phoneNumbers*, violating first normal form. Figure 10.1b satisfies first normal form by placing phone numbers in a separate table and relating them to *OrderItem*.

A table is in *second normal form* if it is in first normal form and all non-primary-key attributes depend on the entire primary key. Figure 10.1b violates second normal form because *orderDatetime*, *customerNumber*, and *emailAddress* depend solely on *orderNumber* and not on *itemNumber*. Figure 10.1c separates *OrderItem* from *Order* and thereby satisfies second normal form.

A table is in *third normal form* when it is in second normal form and each non-primary-key attribute directly depends on the primary key. No attribute can transitively depend on the primary key. Figure 10.1c violates third normal form because there is a transitive dependency — *emailAddress* depends on *customerNumber*, which in turn depends on *orderNumber*. Figure 10.1d places customer data in its own table, satisfying third normal form.

There are additional higher normal forms that are usually not needed in practice.

As Figure 10.1 illustrates, normal forms increase data consistency by separating different kinds of data and placing each in its own table. In general, mixing together different entity

(a) Violates 1st normal form.

OrderItem

orderNumber itemNumber
orderDatetime itemQuantity customerNumber emailAddress phoneNumbers

- -

(b) Satisfies 1st normal form. Violates 2nd normal form.

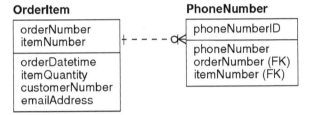

(c) Satisfies 2nd normal form. Violates 3rd normal form.

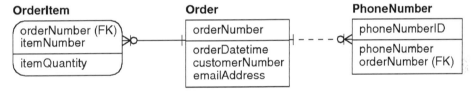

(d) Satisfies 3rd normal form.

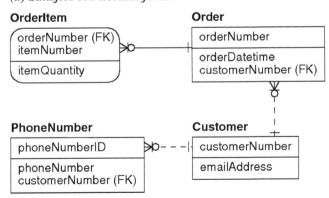

Figure 10.1 Normal forms. A normal form is a guideline for relational
database design that increases data consistency.

types often violates normal forms leading to data quality issues and the inability of the database to accommodate change.

Developers can violate normal forms for good cause, such as to increase performance for a database that is read and seldom updated. Such a relaxation is called **denormalization**. For example, data warehouses are routinely denormalized because users only read data; system-controlled data processing scripts perform the updates. The important issue with normal forms is to violate them deliberately and only when necessary.

Exercises 10.1 and 10.2 can help you verify that you understand normal forms.

10.2 Database Constraints

A sound data model implicitly captures constraints with its structure. That is one of the reasons why we emphasize modeling. However, a model's structure covers only some constraints. You can supplement a model's structure with domain and table constraints.

Chapter 3 discussed domains. Domains not only standardize the assignment of data types, but they also provide a hook for attaching constraints, such as the following:

* quantity > 0

* condition IN ('excellent', 'good', 'fair')

* length (ISBN) = 10 or length (ISBN) = 13

Tables can also have explicit constraints. It is easy to express a constraint among attributes for the same record, such as *expirationDate > effectiveDate*. It is usually impractical to declare constraints across two or more records — application programming is needed to enforce such complex constraints.

Chapter 15 shows how to implement database constraints with SQL check clauses.

10.3 Hillard's Graph Complexity

[Hillard-2010] assesses the quality of a model by measuring its intrinsic complexity. This can also give you a qualitative indication of the effort required to build an application for a model. He equates a data model to an undirected graph. As Figure 10.2 illustrates, an undirected graph consists of nodes (indicated by letters) that are connected by edges (indicated by numbers). There is no sense of direction to the edges; they merely connect nodes.

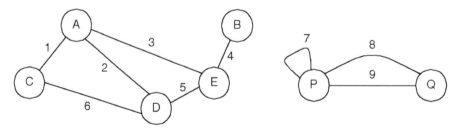

Figure 10.2 Sample undirected graphs. An undirected graph is a
set of nodes and a set of edges that connect the nodes.

With Hillard's approach, a node corresponds to a table and an edge corresponds to a foreign key connection between tables. In UML terms, a node is a class or many-to-many association; an edge is a one-to-one association, a one-to-many association, or a superclass-subclass coupling in a generalization. Hillard has two aspects of complexity. One is the traversal length from one node to another. Models with long traversals are more difficult to understand, more error prone, and more costly to work with. The other aspect is the average number of edges connected to a node. Nodes with three or more edges offer choices leading to decisions about how to traverse from one node to another.

Hillard computes the following graph metrics:

- **Order**. The total number of nodes for the graph.
- **Size**. The total number of edges for the graph.
- **Degree**. The number of edges connected to a node.
- **Geodesic distance**. The minimum number of edges needed to traverse between a pair of nodes.
- **Average degree**. The average number of edges per node for the graph.
- **Average geodesic distance**. The average of the geodesic distance for all node pairs.
- **Maximum geodesic distance**. The maximum geodesic distance for all node pairs.

Figure 10.3 shows a sample model and Figure 10.4 shows the corresponding metrics. Since the metrics are based on an undirected graph, the coupling from *Order* to *Address* counts only once. The order is 5 (5 classes — *Customer*, *Address*, *Order*, *OrderItem*, and *Payment*). The size is also 5 (5 connections between classes — *Order* to *Address*, *Customer* to *Address*, *Customer* to *Order*, *Order* to *OrderItem*, and *Order* to *Payment*).

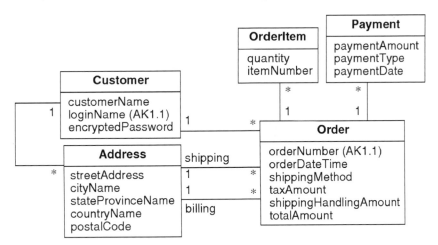

Figure 10.3 Sample data model. You can assess the quality of a model by measuring its traversal complexity.

Consider Figure 10.5. The top model has an average geodesic distance of 1.8 and an average degree of 2. The lower model has an average geodesic distance of 1 but is still complex, because the average degree is 5. Intuitively, the complexity of a model depends on both geodesic distance and degree.

- Order: 5, Size: 5
- Average degree: 2.0 (*Payment*–1, *Order*–4, *Address*–2, *Customer*–2, *Order-Item*–1)
- Average geodesic distance: 1.5
- Maximum geodesic distance: 2

Geodesic distance

	Payment	Order	Address	Customer	OrderItem
Payment	XXX	1	2	2	2
Order	1	XXX	1	1	1
Address	2	1	XXX	1	2
Customer	2	1	1	XXX	2
OrderItem	2	1	2	2	XXX

Figure 10.4 Hillard complexity metrics for Figure 10.3

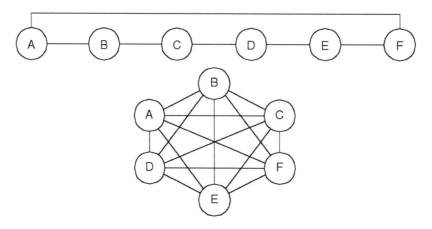

Figure 10.5 Sample graphs. The complexity of a model depends on
both geodesic distance and degree.

Hillard has separate targets for geodesic distance and degree but we prefer to combine them (Figure 10.6). We multiply the geodesic distance by the average degree divided by 3. This combination is consistent with Hillard's advice.

Exercises 10.3, 10.4, and 10.5 can give you practice with Hillard's metrics.

10.4 Hoberman's Data Model Scorecard®

[Hoberman-2009] has created a Data Model Scorecard® for measuring quality, based on his review of hundreds of data models. The scorecard starts with the presumption that the model

---

- **Average geodesic distance * Average degree / 3 <= 4**
  The data model is relatively easy to read and navigate.

- **4 < Average geodesic distance * Average degree / 3 < 10**.
  The data model is complex.

- **10 <= Maximum geodesic distance * Average degree / 3**.
  The data model is effectively unworkable.

Figure 10.6 Data model graph assessment criteria.

is perfect and deducts points where it needs improvement. The scorecard consists of the following items:

1. How well do the characteristics of the model support the type of model? Operational and data warehouse models (two different types of model, see Part 3) must conform to their corresponding architecture. For example, operational models must be normalized (aside from compelling exceptions). Data warehouse models must conform to the star schema.

2. How well does the model capture the requirements? Does the model correctly support the corresponding business processes?

3. How complete is the model? The model should not greatly exceed the requirements to avoid a situation called "scope creep".

4. How structurally sound is the model? For example, primary and alternate keys cannot have null values.

5. How well does the model leverage generic structures? The model should use abstraction and patterns as appropriate.

6. How well does the model follow naming standards?

7. How well has the model been arranged for readability?

8. How good are the definitions?

9. How consistent is the model with the enterprise? An application model should be consistent with an organization's enterprise model.

10. How well does the metadata match the data? For example, do attribute names match the data stored.

Developers quantify compliance for each item and assign a score. This lets the scorecard identify the areas of a model that are solid and those that are lacking. An organization can focus on the low scores and their underlying causes and prepare a plan to remedy defects.

Exercise 10.6 covers preparation of a scorecard.

10.5 Additional Quality Items

We suggest some additional criteria for judging data models:

- **Verify that classes have a crisp theme.** All classes should have a crisp theme to which data must conform. Classes with many attributes are often unwieldy because they mix smaller, more fundamental concepts; in addition, such classes often violate normal forms. A crisp theme is a precondition for good names and definitions.

- **Declare data**. A relational database is supposed to be declarative. For example, a SQL query specifies what is desired and the underlying database platform figures out how to obtain the data. Do not put codes in a database and rely on application programming code to decipher them. Rather put the codes and their definitions in the database.

- **Minimize derived data**. Normally, a model should forego using derived data. (Data warehouses are an exception, as Chapter 13 explains). The reason is that it can be difficult to keep derived data consistent with its underlying data.

- **Minimize redundancy**. Avoid redundancy within applications — store each data item a single time. Also avoid redundancy across applications, where possible. A lack of redundancy across applications is rarely completely feasible as each application has its own timeline, sponsors, and rationale.

- **Keep a model small**. Projects have many pressures that cause a model to grow. As a counterweight, all projects should have an explicit step to consider model removals. Unnecessary content leads to more development work, more time, and more risk.

- **Review models**. Present your models to others to seek their comments and advice. Data models declare the understanding of data so that it can be considered by others. Reviewers can ensure that the model matches their expectations and provide advice.

10.6 Chapter Summary

As you construct data models, it is important to actively work to improve their quality. This chapter covers several techniques: normal forms, database constraints, Hillard's graph complexity, and Hoberman's Data Model Scorecard®. It is not sufficient to construct just any model. Rather you must construct a model of high quality that will support skillful programming and long-term evolution. The quality of a model affects the quality of the data that is stored and the effectiveness of the subsequent applications.

Table 10.1 summarizes the major concepts in this chapter.

Data Modeling Concept	Definition
Normal form	A guideline for relational database design that increases data consistency.
First normal form (for a table)	Each row-column combination of the table stores a single value (and not a collection of values).
Second normal form (for a table)	The table is in first normal form and all non-primary-key attributes depend on the entire primary key.
Third normal form (for a table)	The table is in second normal form and each non-primary-key attribute directly depends on the primary key.
Denormalization (for a table)	A violation of normal forms for good cause, such as when needed for faster performance.

Table 10.1 Terminology summary

Bibliographic Notes

Normal forms are a fundamental aspect of database theory. [Elmasri-2011], [Kent-1983], [Simsion-2005], and [Teorey-2011] explain normal forms in more detail.

References

[Elmasri-2011] Ramez Elmasri and Shamkant B. Navathe. *Fundamentals of Database Systems, Sixth Edition*. Boston: Addison-Wesley, 2011.

[Hillard-2010] Robert Hillard. *Information-Driven Business*. Hoboken, New Jersey: John Wiley, 2010.

[Hoberman-2009] Steve Hoberman. *Data Modeling Made Simple, Second Edition*. Bradley Beach, New Jersey: Technics Publications, 2009.

[Kent-1983] William Kent. A simple guide to five normal forms in relational database theory. *Communications of the ACM 26*, 2 (February 1983), 120–125.

[Simsion-2005] Graeme C. Simsion and Graham C. Witt. *Data Modeling Essentials, Third Edition*. New York: Morgan Kaufmann, 2005.

[Teorey-2011] Toby Teorey, Sam Lightstone, Tom Nadeau, and H.V. Jagadish. *Database Modeling and Design: Logical Design, Fifth Edition*. New York: Morgan Kaufmann, 2011.

Exercises

Each exercise has a difficulty level ranging from 1 (easy) to 10 (very difficult).

10.1 (5) Consider the UML model in Figure E10.1. An example of a conference series is SIGMOD. An example of a conference year is SIGMOD in 2012. Usually, a different person chairs the conference for each year, but it is possible for a person to chair the conference for multiple years. Revise the model so that it is in third normal form. Explain your decisions.

ConferenceYear
seriesFullName
seriesAcronym
seriesWebsite
conferenceYear
conferenceLocation
chairPersonName
chairPersonEmailAddress

Figure E10.1 Conference model to revise

10.2 (5) Revise the model in Figure E10.2 so that it is in third normal form. This is a partial model of data for email messages. Explain your decisions.

10.3 (5) Calculate Hillard metrics for the model in Exercise 3.6.

10.4 (7) Calculate Hillard metrics for the answer to Exercise 5.3.

10.5 (7) Calculate Hillard metrics for the model in Exercise 3.7.

10.6 (8) Prepare a Data Model Scorecard® for the online retail model in Chapter 2.

EmailMessage
emailAccountName emailPassword date subject body sender toRecipients ccRecipients

Figure E10.2 Email model to revise

Test 2

Advanced Modeling Concepts

1. Consider the model in Figure T2.1. Which statement is inconsistent with the model?
   a. A conference has a name, location, start date, and end date.
   b. There are several different offices for a conference (such as program committee, program chair, and general chair) and only one person may serve for each office.
   c. A conference may have multiple calls for papers, each of which has a publication date and describes material that is desired for the conference.
   d. A call for papers lists multiple topics (such as papers, tutorials, and panels) each of which has a name, description, submission date, acceptance date, and a date for submission of final materials.
   e. Each topic can be chaired by many persons.
   f. None of the above.

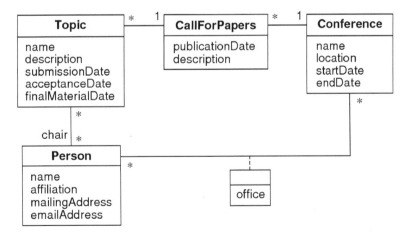

Figure T2.1 Model for a call for papers for a conference

2. Consider the IE models in Figure T2.2. They have different approaches to identity. Are their corresponding UML models the same? The *c_* prefix denotes the migrated key from *CheckingAccount*. The *s_* prefix denotes the migrated key from *Statement*.
    a. Yes
    b. No

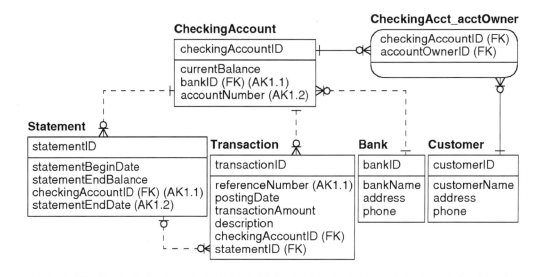

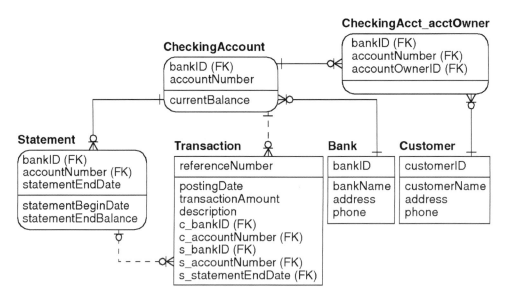

Figure T2.2 Alternate IE checking account models

3. Is it possible for a table to lack a primary key?
    a. Yes
    b. No

4. Do the models in Figure T2.3 describe the same occurrences?
   a. Yes
   b. No

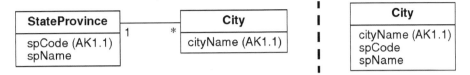

Figure T2.3 Models for address data

5. A developer initially built the model at the top of Figure T2.4 and then restated the model as shown at the bottom. Attribute *movieRole* has the possible values of producer, actor, actress, director, and writer. These models have the same meaning.
   a. True
   b. False

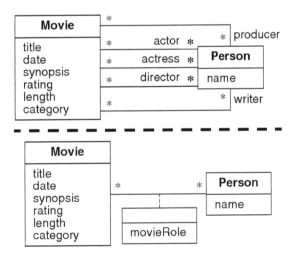

Figure T2.4 Model of movie information

6. Consider the models in Figure T2.5. Both are correct models. Which is the better model?
   a. Left model
   b. Right model

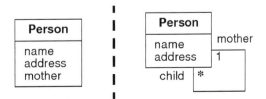

Figure T2.5 Models for persons

7. If you want two links between the same objects, you must have two associations.
    a. True
    b. False

8. Can the top model in Figure 6.7 store the data in Figure T2.6?
    a. Yes
    b. No

> Customer: Joe Brown — Address: 345 Main Street, Boston, MA
> Customer: Joe Brown — Address: 567 Central Street, Boston, MA
> Customer: Sally Smith — Address: 567 Central Street, Boston, MA

Figure T2.6 Sample customer address data

9. Consider the model excerpts shown in Figure T2.7. Which is the better model. Explain your answer.
    a. Top model
    b. Bottom model

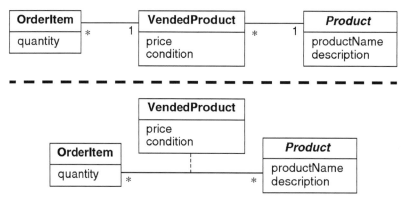

Figure T2.7 Alternative models for VendedProduct

10. Consider the models in Figure T2.8. Both are correct models. Which is the better model?
    a. Left model
    b. Right model

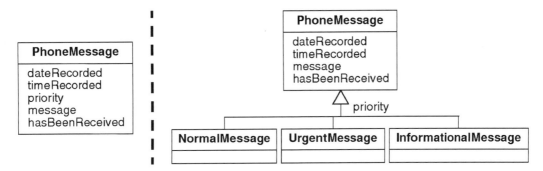

Figure T2.8 Models for phone messages

Part 3

Kinds of Models

Parts 1 and 2 have explained UML data modeling in detail. If you have carefully read the material and worked the exercises and tests, you should be well on your way to constructing UML data models. But there are several kinds of data models that you can construct. They all involve the same building blocks of classes, associations, and attributes, but use them in different ways. Part 3 explains what these kinds of models are and why they are important.

Chapter 11 starts with operational data models. We didn't mention it at the time, but all the examples in Parts 1 and 2 are operational data models. An operational data model concerns the day-to-day needs for running a business. Operational applications process transactions that quickly read and write small amounts of data. It's common to have tens, hundreds, or possibly thousands of transactions per second. Despite this workload, operational applications must correctly update data, even while serving multiple concurrent users.

Chapter 12 explains enterprise data models. An enterprise data model describes the essence of an entire organization or some major aspect of an organization. An enterprise data model standardizes critical concepts across applications, thereby providing a backbone for integrating application data and driving consistency.

Chapter 13 discusses a third kind of data model (analytical data models) — for data warehouses. A data warehouse is a database that is dedicated to data analysis and reporting. A data warehouse acquires data from operational databases and restructures the data so that it can be mined for strategic business insights. Users do not write to a data warehouse; the scripts that load operational data do the writing. Instead users read the warehouse with extensive and complex queries that can take many minutes to run.

Chapter 14 explains master data management. Each master data management deployment focuses on a critical concept and standardizes and cleanses its data, integrating the critical concept across operational applications. This lets an organization establish a "single version of the truth" for critical concepts. An enterprise data model identifies critical concepts that are candidates for master data management.

The self-assessment test can help you judge your comprehension of Part 3.

11

Operational Data Modeling

The first two parts of this book have focused on operational applications — applications that service day-to-day business needs. Most database applications are operational. The databases for operational applications have a web of dependencies among tables that the UML can help to visualize.

11.1 What is an Operational Data Model?

An *operational application* services day-to-day needs for running the business. An operational data model describes the database for an operational application. These applications process many queries that quickly read and write small amounts of data. Examples include payroll processing, order entry, financial trading, and flight reservations.

Many operational applications are performed online, while the user waits, and are referred to as online transaction processing (OLTP). OLTP applications tend to be simple, access few records, and must respond within seconds; they often service forms on a screen for inquiries and data entry.

As with any software, operational applications are vulnerable to development oversights and data entry errors. Nevertheless it is important for their data to be correct, since these applications automate the business. The careful thought behind data models can do much to improve data quality. Operational data models are usually normalized, avoiding redundant and possibly conflicting data. An operational data model can also improve quality by defining referential integrity, as well as uniqueness and miscellaneous constraints.

11.2 Sample Operational Data Model

Chapter 2 presents the online retail data model using the UML and IE notations. This is an example of an operational data model.

11.3 Why Operational Data Models Are Important

Operational data models are important because they specify databases for operational applications. Many of today's business processes are highly automated and rely on computational support. Software makes it possible to perform business processes more efficiently, and furthermore, to perform processes that would not be possible without automation.

Operational applications are not only important for supporting the business routine, but can also enable business change if constructed well. Too many organizations have a business need, construct an application to support the need, and then find themselves locked into a process by software that cannot adapt. Excellent applications look beyond the immediate needs and avoid codifying arbitrary business decisions that might be useful at present, but could change.

11.4 Constructing an Operational Data Model

We begin development of an operational application by preparing a UML data model; we start with a conceptual model and incrementally refine and elaborate it to yield a logical model. We focus on intrinsic classes in a problem and avoid forming "accidental" groups of data. With such a deep basis, the scope of the model can organically grow as the application evolves.

Once a coherent UML model is in place, we then construct an IE data model. Often we must manually rekey the UML model into an IE modeling tool. Automation would be better, but the combination of the UML (good for abstraction and business communication) and IE (good for database design and detailed mechanics) is compelling and worth the additional keystrokes. We document and maintain both models as the application evolves.

As we construct a data model, we consider a wide variety of input sources:

- **Use cases**. A *use case* is a theme for business functionality. Stakeholders should think of the various external entities that interact with the system and the different ways they each use the system. We do not find it necessary to tediously record use cases because a data model can support any number of them. Instead, we note use cases as they arise during business interviews and verify that the model can support them.

- **Business documentation**. Business staff can often provide a statement of motives and intent, screen mock-ups, scenarios, and sample reports. They can also provide definitions for important classes and help clarify multiplicity for associations.

- **Related applications**. You should consider systems that are to be replaced, as well as systems that will remain, but overlap with the new system. Database reverse engineering can recover implicit models from existing systems that are poorly documented.

- **Prior experience**. You may be familiar with the application's subject matter. This can happen when an employee works in a related department or a consultant specializes in a vertical market.

- **Standard models**. Some application models are available from standards organizations. Such models often have wide acceptance. They can save you time and deepen thinking.

We favor agile techniques for constructing data models. With an agile approach, developers work quickly and deliver frequent increments of code. Many persons think of modeling as a laborious task. That need not be the case. (See the *Bibliographic Notes*.)

A data model abridges reality — it describes relevant data for building an application and omits extraneous aspects. However, a data model should not transform reality. A data model should incorporate the nouns and verbs used by the business.

A data model must cover the odd cases. It is the perverse cases that are realistic but seldom occur that stress a data model. You should focus on exceptions, as they can illustrate omissions and flawed representation.

11.5 Chapter Summary

Operational applications serve the day-to-day needs of the business. They execute many queries that read and write small amounts of data. Data modeling is often a pivotal task in building these applications. A data model determines the application's data quality, extensibility, and performance — and influences whether the application has a chance at business success.

Bibliographic Notes

Many persons don't realize that agile data modeling is possible, but this author routinely constructs UML data models with an agile approach. We build the models during live, interactive sessions with business staff. See [Blaha-2011] for a video demonstration.

Norman Daoust gave an interesting talk at the 2012 Data Modeling Zone conference [Daoust-2012]. He divides UML classes into four categories and colors them according to the category. We've used simpler coding schemes ourselves in the past and found that judicious use of color improves model comprehension. The idea that Daoust presented originated with Peter Coad and Jill Nicola.

References

[Blaha-2011] A series of YouTube videos show how to construct UML data models using agile techniques. http://www.youtube.com/view_play_list?p=EE77921A75E846EB

[Daoust-2012] *Modeling the World in Four Colors.* Presentation at Data Modeling Zone conference. Baltimore, Maryland, 2012.

[Coad-1999] Peter Coad, E. Lefebvre, and J. DeLuca, *Java Modeling in Color with UML.* Upper Saddle River, NJ: Prentice Hall PTR, 1999.

[Nicola-2002] Jill Nicola, M. Mayfield, and M. Abney, *Streamlined Object Modeling: Patterns, Rules, and Implementation.* Upper Saddle River, NJ: Prentice Hall PTR, 2002.

12

Enterprise Data Modeling

The most important data is not that which is locked within individual applications, but rather the data which transcends applications and reaches throughout the enterprise. This chapter explains enterprise data models and gives advice for constructing them.

This chapter uses the UML notation alone for enterprise data models and foregoes IE. For an enterprise data model, we prepare a conceptual model and sometimes a simplified logical model. There is no need for the fine detail that comes with the IE notation.

12.1 What Is an Enterprise Data Model?

Typically, most data models are built for a specific application. However, some data transcends applications and does not belong to a single application. Such data can be stored in multiple applications. Without planning and forethought, it can be difficult to understand these repeated copies of data and keep them consistent. Therefore, developers must coordinate individual application databases — this is the purpose of an enterprise data model.

An *enterprise data model (EDM)* describes the essence of an entire organization or some major aspect of an organization. An EDM abstracts multiple applications, combining and reconciling their content. It standardizes critical concepts for an organization and causes consensus. Table 12.1 compares operational (see Chapter 11) and enterprise data models. They differ in their scope, purpose, type of models, use of abstraction, and level of detail:

- **Scope**. An operational model covers a single application. An EDM encompasses multiple applications, for all or part of an organization.

- **Purpose**. The purpose of an operational data model is to specify the data structure for building a database and an application. In contrast, the purpose of an EDM is definitional and does not introduce new data. An EDM provides a basis for reconciling applications and building them in a consistent manner.

- **Type of models**. The EDM has a conceptual model and sometimes a simplified logical model. The cost and difficulty of further elaboration often exceeds the benefits.

	Operational Data Model	**Enterprise Data Model**
Scope	One application.	Multiple applications for all or part of an organization.
Purpose	Build a database that stores data for one application.	Provide a basis for consistent application data.
Type of Models	Has conceptual, logical, and physical models.	Has a conceptual model and sometimes a simplified logical model.
Abstraction	Usually low. Sometimes high.	High. Neutral names rise above the bias of individual applications.
Level of Detail	Must be complete before building an application.	Provides an overview structure to drive consistency. Lacks fine detail.

Table 12.1   Operational data model vs. enterprise data model.
They are much different as the table shows.

- **Abstraction**. Most operational models are straightforward and directly express business concepts. On occasion, an operational model may use deeper abstraction, but the purpose remains to realize specific business goals. By its nature, an EDM is more abstract and rises above the detail of individual applications. An EDM focuses on unifying the deep, underlying concepts.

- **Level of detail**. An operational model must be complete before an application can be built. An EDM, by definition, need not be complete. Rather an EDM provides an overarching perspective for driving consistency across major application concepts. For an organization of any size, it's impractical to construct a full EDM that reconciles all application data. There's too much content to cover. Also, if an EDM includes too much detail, it will be subject to continual rework as constituent applications change.

Ideally, new applications should incorporate the EDM as their starting point. There may be situations where a new application must deviate, but that is not desirable and may, in fact, reflect EDM flaws to fix. Applications can and should elaborate the EDM as needed for their individual purposes.

Legacy applications and purchased applications will, of course, deviate from the EDM. As part of routine maintenance, and consistent with their own product roadmaps, legacy applications should gradually be brought into compliance. Vendor applications, of course, cannot be brought into compliance and should be interfaced to the enterprise model.

12.2 Sample Enterprise Data Model

Figure 12.1 is a first cut at an EDM for online retail. It encompasses applications such as ordering, customer records, and product supply. The *Actor* class covers customer and merchant. *Products* are also prominent. Customers and merchants have *Accounts* and are involved with *Orders*. Section 12.5 defines most of the classes in Figure 12.1. A *VendedProduct* is a *Product* sold by a particular *merchant*; *VendedProducts* for a *Product* can vary in their condition and price.

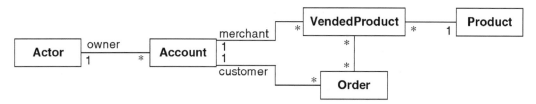

Figure 12.1 Initial EDM for online retail.

12.3 Why Enterprise Data Models Are Important

Enterprise data models are important for several reasons:

- **Organizational vision**. An EDM can deepen understanding of existing applications and help rationalize them. An organization can agree on core names and definitions.

- **Greater data consistency**. Data has greater value when applications are consistent and coherent. An EDM provides a stepping stone for integrating and unifying related applications.

- **Reuse**. Developers can build basic components for the EDM and reuse them in applications. Reusable components are of higher quality than software that is recreated from scratch each time it is needed.

- **Data warehouses**. An EDM is part of the backbone for integrating operational data as a prerequisite for a data warehouse.

12.4 Constructing an Enterprise Data Model

We recommend a two-step process for constructing an EDM:

1. **Reverse engineering**. Start the EDM by infusing application content. Reverse engineer the primary applications to obtain their most important concepts. Use these concepts to seed the initial draft EDM.

    It is important to perform reverse engineering quickly as it is merely an intermediate task on the way to building an enterprise model. The reverse engineering is not a goal in its own right but is a means towards finding important concepts. For seeding an EDM, there is no need to reverse engineer applications in their entirety.

    We favor a simple reverse engineering approach — count incoming and outgoing foreign keys for each application table and include the handful of tables with the highest count. These tables are the initial concepts. Given a modest number of concepts, it usually is not difficult to reconcile the various applications and decide on tentative names and definitions.

    Database design tools, such as ERwin, have some reverse engineering capabilities. The [WCRE] conference series has many informative papers about reverse engineering.

2. **Business review**. Review the draft EDM with business staff to obtain their comments and buy in. Business review also ensures that the model can satisfy future needs not ad-

dressed by current software. In practice, we've found that a series of reviews with small groups works well. You can also tap the knowledge of business reviewers to refine the definitions for EDM concepts.

Reverse engineering ensures that the EDM reflects dominant application concepts. The draft model also seeds business discussions. As we mentioned earlier, an EDM should not attempt to cover every piece of data. You should limit the number of concepts to a dozen or so.

The EDM should be neutral and unbiased by particular applications. Rather, the EDM is a conceptual model for the entire organization. This stands in contrast to an operational data model, which covers only the data for a particular business process.

12.5 Common EDM Concepts

Based on experience with EDM projects over the years, here are concepts that often arise. [Blaha-2010] explains many of these concepts further and shows data model excerpts:

- **Account**. A label for recording, reporting, and managing associated data.
- **Activity**. Behavior that can be performed. This includes historical activity as well as scheduled activity yet to occur.
- **Actor**. Someone or something that is notable in terms of data or relationships. Includes persons and organizations, as well as roles and role types.
- **Asset**. Something of value.
- **Contract**. An agreement for the supply of products and services.
- **Document**. A physical or electronic representation of a body of information.
- **Equipment**. Tools and machinery needed to complete activities. Equipment is used, but not consumed by activities.
- **Event**. An occurrence at a point in time.
- **Location**. A physical or logical place in space.
- **Order**. A request for delivery of a product or service.
- **Product**. The packaging of a product or service for a marketplace.
- **Transaction**. An exchange that must be completed in its entirety or not at all.

12.6 Chapter Summary

An enterprise data model (EDM) is a data model that describes the essence of an organization. An EDM abstracts multiple applications, combining and reconciling their content. Ideally, new applications should take advantage of the EDM as their starting point. Legacy applications and purchased applications will, of course, deviate from the EDM. As part of routine maintenance, legacy applications should gradually be brought into compliance. Vendor applications cannot be brought into compliance and should be interfaced to the enterprise model.

We recommend a two-step process for constructing an EDM. Start by reverse engineering the primary applications to obtain their most important concepts and seed the initial draft

EDM. As a second step, review the draft EDM with business staff to obtain their refinements, comments, and buy in.

Bibliographic Notes

[Hillard-2010] estimates that roughly 50% of a company's value derives from its data. This means that a company with a market value of $10 billion has $5 billion in information and knowledge assets, including intellectual property. Given this context, an enterprise model can be an important investment.

References

[Blaha-2010] Michael Blaha. *Patterns of Data Modeling*. New York: CRC Press. 2010.

[Hillard-2010] Robert Hillard. *Information-Driven Business*. New York: John Wiley. 2010.

[WCRE] There has been a series of *Working Conferences on Reverse Engineering* dating back twenty years now. This is a great resource for all facets of reverse engineering, including databases. You can find more information about the WCRE conferences by searching the Web on 'WCRE'.

Exercises

Each exercise has a difficulty level ranging from 1 (easy) to 10 (very difficult).

12.1 (8) Figure E12.1 shows a model for Canadian customs data. Assume that a database accumulates customs data over time. Each declaration form has space for multiple persons. The model presumes that the database must resolve multiple declarations to the same person record (and not repeatedly store person data). The purpose of a trip is study, personal, or business. The arrival source is the USA only, other country direct, or other country via the USA. The farm country indicates if a person has been on a non-Canadian farm during the past 14 days. The general customs questions seemed arbitrary and subject to future change so the model captures them as generic questions and answers. The form has different data for visitors than for residents.

The answer to Exercise 4.12 shows a model for USA customs data. In principle, the forms of both countries are trying to achieve the same purpose. Nevertheless, the models vary because of the different data content of Canadian and American forms, as well as different modeling representations.

Suppose we have an information system that must be able to handle both kinds of forms. For example, Canada and the USA may exchange customs data for security purposes. Prepare a model that combines the Canadian and American models.

Another way of looking at this problem is that the Canadian customs declaration model is one application and the American customs declaration model is another application. This exercise is asking you to construct a model that combines the two applications. Such a combined model would be a precursor to an enterprise data model.

12.2 (5) Consider the model for the auto insurance card for the answer to Exercise 4.11. Figure E12.2 shows a model for an auto insurance bill. Prepare an enterprise conceptual model that covers the two applications. In the enterprise conceptual model, you should have three classes: *Person, InsurancePolicy,* and *PhysicalVehicle.* Do not show any attributes or detailed classes in your answer.

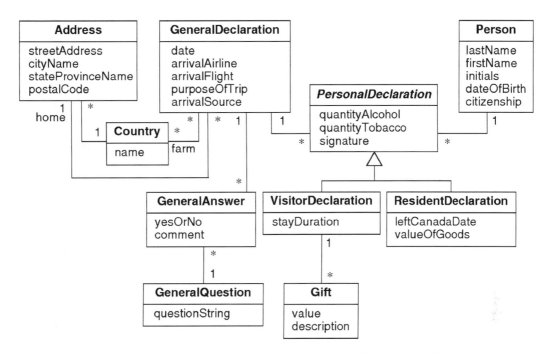

Figure E12.1 Model to handle data from Canadian customs forms

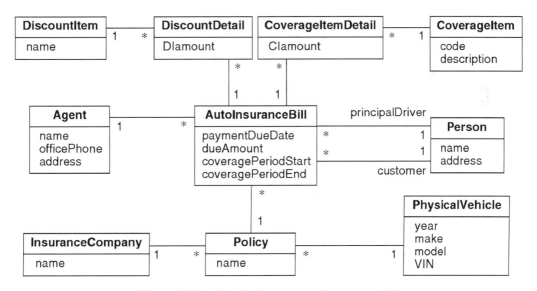

Figure E12.2 Model for an auto insurance bill

13

Data Warehouses

A data warehouse is a database that accumulates data from the day-to-day operational systems and serves the needs of decision support. This chapter explains data warehouse models and how they differ from operational data models.

This chapter uses the IE notation alone for modeling data warehouses and foregoes the UML. Data warehouses have a simple structure and there is no benefit to using the UML. A database notation is sufficient for both modeling and database design.

13.1 What Is a Data Warehouse?

A *data warehouse* is a database that is dedicated to data analysis and reporting. It combines data from multiple operational applications (see Chapter 11) and provides one location for decision-support data. A data warehouse places data on a common basis—for the same period, same geographical area, and same currency. For example, there is one copy of each customer and their data.

Data warehouses are structured as facts that store data for some combination of dimensions. Such an architecture provides ease of use as well as good performance. A *fact* measures the performance of a business. Sample facts include sales, budget, revenue, profit, inventory, and return on investment. A *dimension* specifies a basis for facts. Sample dimensions include date, customer, location, product, account, and supplier. The data modeling paradigm of a fact surrounded by multiple dimensions is called a *star schema*.

Data warehouses receive data from periodic loading. System scripts read operational data and write to data warehouses. Data warehouses not only store source data, but also maintain history through successive data loads. Users do not write to a data warehouse.

Table 13.1 compares operational applications with data warehouses. Operational applications are often called OLTP (online transaction processing). Data warehouses are often called OLAP (online analytical processing):

- **Purpose**. Operational applications focus on day-to-day business needs. These applications perform routine tasks such as processing orders, procuring supplies, and making payroll. Data warehouses take the data from operational applications and use it for an-

	Operational Application (OLTP)	Data Warehouse (OLAP)
Purpose	Support day-to-day operation of the business.	Glean strategic business insights from data.
Structure	A complex graph of relationship types connect entity types.	Facts are surrounded by dimensions that can be shared.
Data History	Usually just current data.	Accumulates history via periodic operational data loads.
Reading	Usually a few records at a time.	Can involve billions of records.
Writing	Updated by users as part of business processes.	Updated by periodic loads of operational data.
Response Time	Often is sub-second.	Often can take many minutes to run.
Data Integrity	Normalized data. Referential integrity. Applications check for errors.	Denormalized data. No referential integrity. System data loads check for errors.
Locking	Access few records at a time to minimize locking contention.	Schedule data loads at times that do not contend with queries.

Table 13.1   Operational application vs. data warehouse. They are much different as the table shows.

other purpose — decision support. The data that is captured during routine tasks is a wealth of data that can be restructured and mined for strategic benefit.

- **Structure**. Operational applications have a complex graph of related entity types. In contrast, analytical applications have a simpler structure; facts are surrounded by dimensions that can be shared.

- **Data history**. Typically, operational applications store only the most current data. For example, a price update may overwrite the past price and only the current price is stored. Data warehouses differ in that they often capture the history of changes that occur over time. For example, a data warehouse might track the price history along with effective and expiration dates.

- **Reading**. Most operational applications process small amounts of data (a few records at a time). Data warehouse queries can involve billions of records or more.

- **Writing**. Users update operational databases as part of the business routine. In contrast, system scripts (ETL — Extract, Transform, and Load — scripts) write to data warehouses. ETL scripts post new data at periodic, scheduled times.

- **Response time**. Many operational applications process transactions with a sub-second response. In contrast, lengthy data warehouse queries can take many minutes to run.

- **Data integrity**. Properly designed operational applications normalize data for all but the most urgent circumstances. Operational applications have frequent small updates and referential integrity can compensate for some errors and oversights. In contrast, data warehouse applications routinely denormalize; data warehouse system scripts have the responsibility for keeping redundant data consistent.

- **Locking**. Since operational applications have ongoing reading and writing, locking contention is a concern. Operational applications typically access only a few records at a time to minimize conflicts. Data warehouses often limit their updates to off hours. Then during busy times, there is only reading and no writing.

13.2 Sample Data Warehouse Model

Figure 13.1 shows a sample data warehouse model. We have recast data from the operational model in Chapter 2 into data warehouse form. Each data warehouse dimension has a primary key that is a surrogate key (suffix of *key*), apart from the natural key (suffix of *ID*) in the operational applications. A data warehouse has keys in addition to IDs because there can be a history of data and descriptive attributes may change over time for the same ID.

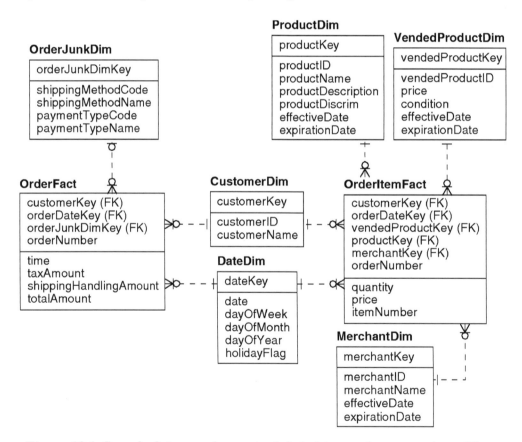

Figure 13.1 Sample data warehouse model. A data warehouse consists of facts that refer to dimensions. Dimensions are conformed across facts.

In Figure 13.1, order facts relate to customer and date. In addition, a junk dimension (a dimension consisting of miscellaneous codes and strings, see Section 13.6) covers shipping method and payment type. Order item facts relate to customer, date, product, vended product, and merchant. The *orderNumber* is a degenerate dimension consisting of nothing but the attribute. Consequently, it is sufficient to store *orderNumber* in the facts and not create another dimension table. The model shows only some of the attributes. Several dimensions maintain a history of data and accordingly have effective and expiration dates. Queries include the following:

- Do orders vary by day of the week?
- Are orders affected by holidays?
- Which customers placed the most orders in the past year?
- Does the choice of a shipping method correlate with the size of an order?
- What is the average price of each merchant's offerings?

13.3 Why Data Warehouses Are Important

Data warehouses are important for many reasons:

- **Business insight**. Operational data has more value than just supporting day-to-day tasks. The data is a rich resource for analysis.
- **Historical trends**. A data warehouse can store data history, even if source systems do not. A data warehouse provides the wherewithal for discovering trends.
- **Understandability**. The star schema is a simple structure that is conducive to posing queries. In contrast, most operational databases have a complex structure for which a user interface must mediate access.
- **Greater efficiency**. The data warehouse is a separate database that handles analytical queries so that they do not interfere with day-to-day operational tasks. Data warehouses minimize their own lock contention by carefully scheduling updates.
- **Improved data consistency**. A data warehouse integrates data from its source systems and places the data on a consistent basis.

13.4 Constructing a Data Warehouse

There are two philosophies about how to construct a data warehouse, Inmon and Kimball.

The Inmon approach is to prepare a detailed enterprise model that integrates the underlying operational applications and then use the detailed enterprise model as the basis for constructing a data warehouse. The enterprise model can be constructed in its entirety or built incrementally as a data warehouse proceeds. Kimball takes a different perspective and constructs portions of a data warehouse as business needs arise.

We favor Kimball's approach for two reasons. First, it is difficult and failure-prone to construct Inmon's detailed enterprise data model. (Recall that in Chapter 12 we discouraged construction of a detailed enterprise model.) Second, Kimball's business-driven approach is more consistent with agile development.

It is a good practice to build data warehouses with a bus architecture — a *bus architecture* consists of dimensions that are consistently defined for reuse across facts. This kind of rigorous modeling increases data consistency and enables queries across facts. For example, we could compare data for *OrderItemFacts* to *OrderFacts*. A bus architecture also helps with incrementally building and populating tables. Facts will share many dimensions for a correctly modeled data warehouse.

Data warehouses can be subdivided into **data marts** that store subsets of data, often for a particular purpose. Since a data mart has a smaller scope, it can be built more quickly and realize faster payback. Often a data mart is built to satisfy the needs of a department. The data marts must eventually be able to combine into a data warehouse, so developers must make sure that dimensions conform.

A data warehouse for a large organization will typically have 10–25 fact tables. Each fact will have 5–15 dimensions [Kimball-2008]. If there are too few dimensions, you probably need to think more deeply about possible queries and different aspects of data. If there are too many dimensions, some of the dimensions are probably not independent, and you should combine them.

A data warehouse model should avoid premature summarization of facts because it limits queries. Instead, model facts with the lowest level of detail and add summaries only as needed.

13.5 Facts

A *fact* measures the performance of a business. Examples include price, budget, revenue, profit, inventory, and return on investment. Queries often summarize facts by aggregating one or more of the associated dimensions. The *grain* of a fact is the lowest level of detail for which records may be defined. A fact table should have a uniform grain. For example, a fact table should not mix transactional data with summary data.

Facts should have numeric measurements (and not strings) so that queries can summarize them. There are three kinds of numeric values that a fact can store:

- **Additive**. Measures that can be added across any dimension. For example, revenue can be added across different products.

- **Semi additive**. Measures that can be added across some dimensions or at certain levels within a dimension, Cash balance can be added across accounts but cannot be added across time (such as for the different days in a week).

- **Non additive**. Measures that cannot be added across any dimension. Ratios, percentages, and more complex calculations (such as return on investment) are usually not additive.

There are also three kinds of facts:

- **Transactional**. This is the most basic kind of fact and has one row for each transaction, or one row for each summarization of transactions. For example, there would be one row for each line number of an order. The data is detailed, so there are often many associated dimensions.

- **Periodic snapshot**. These fact tables summarize transactional data for a time interval. For example, there could be periodic snapshots summarizing orders for each month of the year. A periodic snapshot is computed from detailed data in a transactional fact table.

- **Accumulating snapshot**. This kind of fact table measures progress as something is managed with a business process. For example, there could be an accumulating snapshot monitoring the progress of order processing steps. As each step is completed, the associated fact row is updated.

It is possible to have a fact table without measures. A *factless fact* lacks measures and solely denotes the presence of the relationship types to the dimensions. Factless fact tables can be useful for modeling many-to-many relationship types and capturing events.

13.6 Dimensions

A *dimension* is a concept or thing that provides a basis for facts. Examples include date, customer, location, product, account, and supplier. A dimension has descriptive attributes that are useful for filtering records in queries, grouping records in queries, and labeling reports. In a proper data warehouse, dimensions are standardized (conformed) so that they apply to multiple facts. For example, a data warehouse should have one copy of customer that applies across all facts.

As Figure 13.2 shows, most dimensions store only current values (Kimball type 1) or are *slowly changing* and store a history of values (Kimball type 2). For example, in the left model, *CustomerDim* has only a name and is type 1. In the right model, *CustomerDim* is type 2. For example, John Doe could have billing address 123 Main Street from January 1, 2005 through January 1, 2009 and 456 State Street from January 1, 2009 through the present. Type 2 dimensions keep a history of data and each record is valid for some time interval.

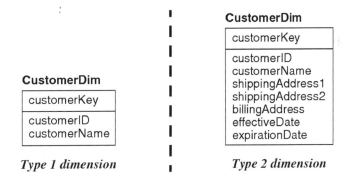

Figure 13.2 Dimensions. Most dimensions store only current values (Kimball type 1) or are slowly changing and store a history of values (Kimball type 2).

A *conformed dimension* is a dimension that is cleanly defined for reuse across facts. A fact may have multiple references (**roles**) to the same dimension. For example, the *OrderFact* table could have both a *billingDate* and a *shippingDate*. Important conformed dimensions can often be found in an enterprise data model.

A *junk dimension* is an arbitrary grouping of flags, codes, and strings. For example, we placed the shipping method code, shipping method name, payment type code, and payment type name in the *OrderJunkDim* dimension. Logically, these attributes belong to an order, but are omitted from the fact table to reduce record size and improve performance. A junk dimension should have several orders of magnitude fewer records than a fact table. It would be possible to have a separate table for each of the four attributes, but then the fact table would have four foreign keys instead of the one junk foreign key. Junk dimension attributes need not correlate.

There are two ways of populating a junk dimension. One way is to store combinations of junk attributes as they are encountered. For example, a new *OrderJunkDim* record would be created for each new combination of shipping method code, shipping method name, payment type code, and payment type name. The other way is to load all possibilities in advance. Chapter 2 lists nine possible combinations — shipping method of post office, UPS, and Fed Ex, as well as payment type of credit card, check, and money order. Prepopulation is convenient if there is a modest number of records that are known in advance or there is a need to validate against a predetermined set of values. Otherwise, incremental junk loading is a better technique.

A *degenerate dimension* is a dimension that has an identifier but no other descriptive attributes. It need not have a dimension table and can be stored as an attribute in one or more fact tables. For example, *orderNumber* is a degenerate dimension.

A *snowflake structure* results when a dimension is normalized and split into multiple tables. For example, the product dimension in the online retail example could be elaborated with a product category. Snowflakes complicate a data warehouse and are usually unnecessary. Most dimension tables are small compared with fact tables. You should consider snowflakes only for monster dimensions with many records that occupy 10 percent or more of the overall data warehouse disc space.

13.7 Chapter Summary

Data warehouse applications are built to service complex queries that read large amounts of data and glean insights. A data warehouse integrates the data from one or more operational applications, accumulates a history of the data over time, and uses this data to support analyses. Table 13.2 summarizes the major concepts in this chapter.

Bibliographic Notes

Inmon and Kimball have both written excellent books about data warehouses. Section 13.4 summarizes their approaches.

A data warehouse has a low Hillard complexity score, as Exercise 13.4 illustrates.

References

[Hillard-2010] Robert Hillard. *Information-Driven Business*. Hoboken, New Jersey: John Wiley, 2010.

[Inmon-2005] William H Inmon. *Building the Data Warehouse, Fourth Edition*. New York: Wiley-QED, 2005.

[Kimball-2008] Ralph Kimball, Laura Reeves, Margy Ross, Warren Thornthwaite, and Joy Mundy. *The Data Warehouse Lifecycle Toolkit, Second Edition*. New York: Wiley, 2008.

Data Modeling Concept	Definition
Bus architecture	A data warehouse approach for which dimensions are consistently defined for reuse across facts.
Data mart	Part of a data warehouse that addresses a specific purpose.
Data warehouse	A database that is dedicated to data analysis and reporting.
Dimension	A concept or thing that provides a basis for facts. A dimension has descriptive attributes that are useful for filtering records in queries, grouping records in queries, and labeling reports.
Dimension, conformed	A dimension that is cleanly defined for reuse across facts.
Dimension, degenerate	A dimension that has an identifier but no other descriptive attributes.
Dimension, junk	An arbitrary grouping of flags, codes, and strings.
Dimension, slowly changing	A dimension that stores a history of values (Kimball type 2).
Fact	Measures the performance of a business. Facts should have numeric values (and not strings) so that queries can summarize them.
Fact, factless	A fact that lacks measures and solely denotes the presence of the relationship types to the dimensions.
Grain (of a fact)	The lowest level of detail for which records may be defined.
Role	A reference from a fact to a dimension. A fact can have multiple references to the same dimension.
Snowflake structure	A dimension that is split into multiple tables.
Star schema	The data modeling paradigm of a fact surrounded by multiple dimensions.

Table 13.2 Terminology summary

Exercises

Each exercise has a difficulty level ranging from 1 (easy) to 10 (very difficult).

13.1 (8) Start with the answer to Exercise 8.2. Create a data warehouse model with fact tables for *AuctionItemFact*, *WatchFact*, and *BidFact*.

13.2 (6) Modify *ItemDim* from the answer to the previous exercise so that it snowflakes on *ItemCategory*.

13.3 (6) Consider the answer to Exercise 5.4 and assume that the subclasses have more attributes than the answer shows. There are three possibilities for a data warehouse model.

- A single fact for transaction.
- Multiple facts, only for the subclasses (deposit, transfer, debit, check, interest, fee).
- Facts for transaction as well as the subclasses (seven facts in all).

Figure E13.1 shows a data warehouse model for *TransactionFact* (the first option). Which of the three options do you consider to be the best. Explain your rationale.

13.4 (5) Compute Hillard quality metrics for Figure 13.1,

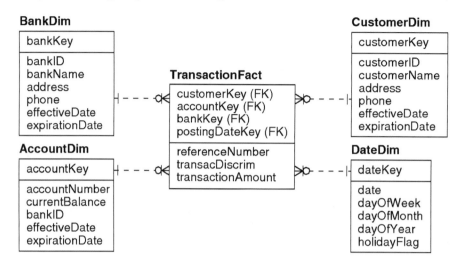

Figure E13.1 Transaction data warehouse — first option

14

Master Data Modeling

Like enterprise data modeling (Chapter 12), master data modeling is also aimed at improving the enterprise. Enterprise data modeling takes the perspective of synchronizing multiple key concepts across the enterprise. Master data modeling takes a different perspective, focusing on just one key concept and synchronizing it, as well as its detailed data across the enterprise.

14.1 What is a Master Data Model?

Master data management (*MDM*) focuses on a critical concept for an organization and standardizes and cleanses its data (attributes, associations, and closely related classes) across applications. This lets an organization establish a "single version of the truth" for critical concepts. MDM does not fix all the ills of disjointed applications, but it materially helps. If data for a critical concept is unified across applications, part of the application integration puzzle is solved and the remaining problem is simplified. [Berson-2011] claims that bringing order to master data often solves 60-80% of the most critical and difficult-to-fix data quality problems. [Berson-2011] projects that 80% of Fortune 5000 companies have committed to MDM as a core business strategy as of 2012.

Conflicting data across applications is a problem for almost every enterprise. There is too much data to try to standardize every piece. MDM presumes that some data (master concepts) are more important than the rest. MDM fixes data for critical concepts and defers work for less important data.

If there are multiple critical concepts to standardize, then there can be multiple MDM deployments. For example, there could be one MDM system to standardize customer data and another MDM system to standardize product data. Most MDM software is written generically so that it can be tailored to any critical concept.

14.2 Sample Master Data Model

Figure 14.1 and Figure 14.2 show an initial customer master data model for the online retail application using the UML and IE notations. We have added data not shown in Chapter 2.

The example presumes that additional applications access customer data. We do not show history for any of the classes, as history seems unimportant for online retail. *Membership* refers to membership in special marketing groups, such as for students and military families. *Preference* handles email and notification options that a customer can set. *PaymentMethod* usually refers to a credit or debit card. The model has two address classes so that it is easy to edit addresses.

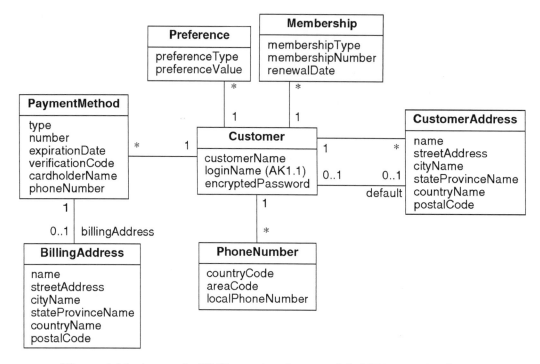

Figure 14.1 A sample UML master data model. MDM standardizes and cleanses data for a critical concept across applications.

14.3 Why Master Data Models Are Important

Master data models are important for many reasons:

- **Greater data consistency**. MDM unifies data across applications. MDM is a stepping stone towards application integration.

- **Economical data cleansing**. MDM focuses on cleansing data with high impact. This is more economical than cleaning all the data.

- **Faster development**. The cleansed and coherent data from an MDM project provides a nucleus for seeding new applications.

- **Data warehouses**. Clean operational data is a data warehouse prerequisite. MDM sanitizes data for a data warehouse dimension.

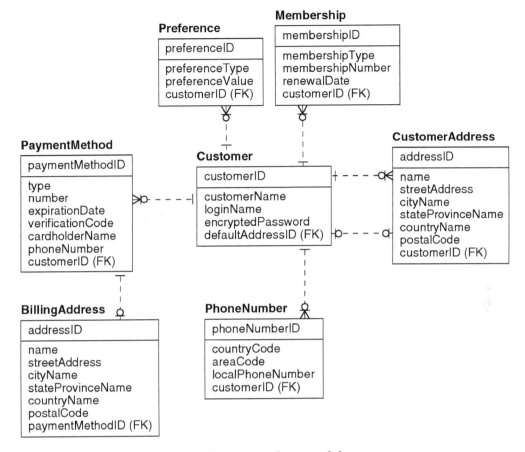

Figure 14.2 A sample IE master data model

14.4 Constructing a Master Data Model

We recommend the following high-level process for constructing a master data model:

1. **Determine the focus**. Determine the critical concept that is the MDM focus, such as customer, product, account, or location.

2. **Flesh out the data model**. Prepare a data model for the critical concept, adding attributes and related classes. Normally a master data model has one-to-many and one-to-one relationship types that radiate out from the critical concept.

3. **Consider existence dependency**. Consider existence dependency in setting multiplicity for the parent. For example, a *Preference* record depends on a *Customer* record; if the *Customer* record is deleted, so too is the *Preference*. We split address into *CustomerAddress* and *BillingAddress* so that some address records can be owned by *Customer* and others by *PaymentMethod*.

14.5 Operational Data Modeling and MDM

MDM source data comes from operational applications, but MDM differs from operational data modeling in that it spans applications and has a limited focus. Master classes cut across multiple operational applications and serve as touch points for integration.

14.6 Enterprise Data Modeling and MDM

MDM is a complementary technology to enterprise data modeling (EDM). An MDM deployment standardizes detailed data for a critical concept. In contrast, EDM elicits all the high level concepts for an organization and standardizes them (and not their detailed data). The critical concepts that EDM identifies are candidates for detailed work with MDM. Both MDM and EDM aim to reduce inconsistency across an organization while trying not to fix all data at once. Table 14.1 has a further comparison.

	Master Data Model	**Enterprise Data Model**
Scope	Multiple applications for all or part of an organization.	Multiple applications for all or part of an organization.
Focus	One core concept and its ancillary data.	A handful of the core, most important concepts.
Purpose	Promote consistent application data.	Promote consistent application data.
Type of Models	Has conceptual, logical, and physical models.	Has a conceptual model and sometimes a simplified logical model.
Abstraction	Moderate. Neutral names rise above the bias of individual applications but there is detailed data.	High. Neutral names rise above the bias of individual applications and there are only critical concepts.
Size	One critical concept. Generally no more than a few dozen detailed classes.	A handful of critical concepts.

Table 14.1 Master data model vs. enterprise data model. There is much similarity between these two technologies.

14.7 Data Warehouses and MDM

MDM also compliments data warehouses. MDM standardizes data for a critical concept. A critical concept is used throughout an organization and manifests as a major dimension in a data warehouse. An MDM effort is often a stepping-stone to a data warehouse. MDM rationalizes the multiple copies of a critical concept that exist across applications and makes them consistent.

14.8 Chapter Summary

Master data management (MDM) focuses on a critical concept for an organization and standardizes and cleanses its data (attributes, associations, and closely related classes) across applications. MDM does not fix all the ills of disjointed applications, but it materially helps. If data for a critical concept is unified across applications, part of the application integration puzzle is solved, and the remaining problem is simplified.

MDM presumes that some data (that for master concepts) is more important than the rest. MDM fixes data for critical concepts and defers work for less important data.

Bibliographic Notes

[Berson-2011] thoroughly explains MDM technology and how to succeed with MDM projects.

References

[Berson-2011] Alex Berson and Larry Dubov. *Master Data Management and Data Governance*. New York: McGraw-Hill, 2011.

Exercises

Each exercise has a difficulty level ranging from 1 (easy) to 10 (very difficult).

14.1 (9) Prepare a master data model for online retail product data. Since there is a wide variety of products, one approach is to abstract products with metadata.

14.2 (8) The U.S. census has different kinds of locations: street address, city, census designated place, county, state province, region, and country. Data that is captured includes: name, geo coordinates, time zone, and parent location. Prepare a master data model for location.

Test 3
Kinds of Models

1. Consider Figure T3.1. How would you categorize this model? The boxes denote classes. The model does not show class names or attributes, but you can see how classes connect via associations. Explain your answer.
   a. Operational data model
   b. Enterprise data model
   c. Data warehouse
   d. Master data model

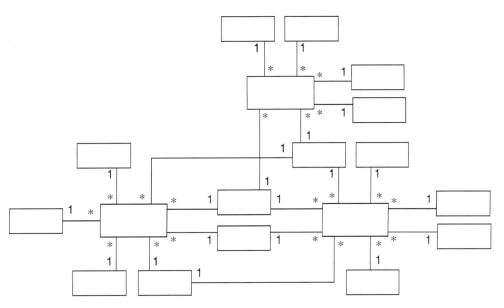

Figure T3.1 A data model

2. Consider Figure T3.2. How would you categorize this model? Explain your answer.
    a. Operational data model
    b. Enterprise data model
    c. Data warehouse
    d. Master data model

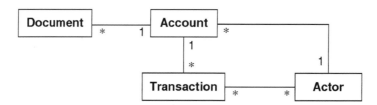

Figure T3.2 A data model

3. What kinds of data models can reasonably have fifty or more classes. This question may have more than one answer. Explain your answer(s).
    a. Operational data model
    b. Enterprise data model
    c. Data warehouse
    d. Master data model

4. What kinds of data models need not have referential integrity enforced by the database. This question may have more then one answer. Explain your answer(s).
    a. Operational data model
    b. Enterprise data model
    c. Data warehouse
    d. Master data model

5. Why is it important that the dimensions of a data warehouse be conformed? This question may have more than one answer. Explain your answer(s).
    a. To reduce the number of tables in a data warehouse.
    b. So that queries on different facts can be compared against each other.
    c. So that there is a single version of the truth in the data warehouse.
    d. None of the above.

Part 4

Database Design

Part 4 concludes the book and shows how to take data models and use them for design. First you create the code for the initial empty database structure. You can also use the data model as a guide for writing database queries.

Chapter 15 covers the design of database structure. You start with the UML and IE data models and make any final adjustments. Now is the time to fine tune the precise physical tables, as well as check the assignment of domains and data types. Normally every table should have a primary key, and you should also define alternate keys, as appropriate. Other items to consider are indexes, referential integrity, check constraints, and views. The ultimate result is a SQL script that creates the initial empty database structure.

Chapter 16 takes a different perspective of a data model — as a guide for converting business logic into SQL queries. The Object Constraint Language (OCL) is a textual language that is another one of the multiple notations that comprise the UML. The OCL is intended for expressing constraints, but is also suitable for expressing class model traversals. You should start with a business statement of intent and write the corresponding OCL logic. Don't worry if the OCL logic is a bit rough, as we are only using it as a guide for writing SQL code. The backbone of most SQL queries is a series of joins (inner and outer joins) that correspond to class model traversals.

The self-assessment test can help you judge your comprehension of Part 4.

15

Database Structure

We have explained how to construct data models using a blend of the UML and IE notations. Developers start with a conceptual model of intent and add attributes and detailed classes to obtain a logical model. The physical model then adds database design decisions to the logical model.

For any serious database design, developers should use a tool. It is tedious and error prone to manually write SQL statements to create tables and ancillary data structures.

15.1 Fine Tuning of Physical Tables

IE makes it clear which tables are generated; each entity type box leads to a SQL table. If your application needs fine tuning, you can adjust the IE diagram. (However, such table optimization is seldom necessary; SQL is efficient if you follow the rules in this chapter.)

Table partitioning is an example of table optimization. In Figure 15.1, a table can split horizontally or vertically into lesser tables. Vertical partitioning is helpful when attributes have different access rules. For example, a person's protected health attributes (such as name and social security number) must be secured, but anonymous attributes (such as height, weight, and blood type) are less sensitive. Horizontal partitioning is useful when some records have much different access frequency than others.

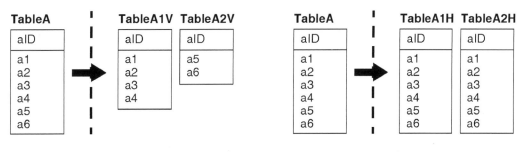

Vertical Partitioning   *Horizontal Partitioning*

Figure 15.1 Table partitioning. You can split a logical table into
lesser physical tables.

We rename *Order* to *OrderTable* to avoid violating a SQL keyword.

15.2 Domains and Data Types

Earlier, in Chapter 3, we discussed domains and data types. A *domain* is the named set of possible values for an attribute. A *data type* specifies the type and size for values. If you have not already done so, you need to specify the domain or data type for each attribute. Most database design tools have excellent support for domains and data types.

An *enumeration domain* limits attribute values to a finite list of choices. Enumeration domains have several design options:

- **Enumeration string**. Store an enumeration attribute as a string. For example, *shippingMethod* would have the possible values 'post office, 'UPS', or 'Fed Ex'. A SQL check constraint can ensure there are no misspellings and that values conform to the list. This is a good approach when there are only a few enumeration values that seldom change.

- **One flag per enumeration value**. Use multiple attributes to cover the possibilities. The earlier example would have three boolean attributes: *isPostOfficeShipped*, *isUpsShipped*, and *isFedExShipped*. A SQL check constraint could ensure that no more than one of these flags was true. This approach clearly displays the possible values in the database structure. This approach is also effective when enumeration values are not mutually exclusive and multiple values can simultaneously apply.

- **Enumeration table**. One or more special tables define enumeration codes and values. You could have one table for each enumeration or one table that stores all enumerations. This can be a good option for an application with many enumerations. The advantage is that the database declares enumerations so that they are clearly visible and uniform within an application.

- **Enumeration encoding**. Database tables store each enumeration as a code. For example, the *shippingMethod* might be 1, 2, or 3. Application programming would then perform the decoding. This is a poor approach. A database should be self contained and not dependent on application programming for its meaning.

Null is a special value denoting an attribute value that is unknown or not applicable. As an example, the *shippingMethod* for each *Order* record in the online retail model has the possible values: 'post office', 'UPS', 'Fed Ex', or NULL. The SQL create table command permits attributes to be null. When this is not satisfactory, you can specify particular attributes as *not null*. Alternatively, you can specify a default value. For example, if the user does not specify a *shippingMethod*, it may default to 'post office'.

15.3 Primary and Alternate Keys

First, let us review some definitions from Chapter 6. A *candidate key* is a combination of one or more attributes that uniquely identifies each record within a table. The attributes in a candidate key must be minimal. No attribute in a candidate key can be null. A *primary key* is an arbitrary choice of candidate key that is used for foreign key references. A table can have at most one primary key and normally should have one. An *alternate key* is a candidate key that is not chosen as a primary key. Therefore each candidate key is either a primary key or an alternate key.

Verify that you have defined primary keys throughout your model. Also look for additional unique combinations of attributes to enforce as alternate keys. For the online retail example, *OrderItem* has a primary key of *orderItemID* and an alternate key of *orderID + itemNumber*.

If you are using existence-based identity, as we favor in this book, keep in mind that most databases can generate new identifiers. For example, Oracle has a sequence number generator and SQL Server has the identity data type. A database design tool will expose this capability and make it available.

15.4 Indexes

Indexes provide the primary means for tuning most relational databases. An *index* is an auxiliary data structure that locates records according to table column values. For example, a phone book is effectively indexed on last name + first name so that you can quickly find persons within a metropolitan area. It is much faster to go to the phone book (an indexed search), than to search through a phone number list (a sequential search), until you find the desired name.

An index is typically implemented as an inverted tree with a wide fan-out at each node (often a factor of 50 or more). An index improves table reading at the cost of slower writes and increased storage space. When properly used, indexes can speed reading by multiple orders of magnitude. An index typically slows the writing of records by 20-30%. Indexes can be created on one or more columns, providing both fast random lookups and efficient ordered access of records.

There are several kinds of indexes:

- **Unique index**. An index which enforces that a combination of attributes is unique and can never repeat. Most relational databases create unique indexes as a side effect of SQL primary key and unique (alternate key) constraints.

- **Non-unique index**. A combination of attributes may occur repeatedly.

- **Clustered index**. The index physically orders table records. As you might expect, a table has, at most, one clustered index as it can have only one ordering. Clustered indexes can make database joins very fast, as the next chapter explains.

You should build an index for each foreign key that is not subsumed by a primary key or alternate key constraint. Some database design tools can generate an index for every foreign key. You can also define indexes for other combinations of attributes that are frequently accessed. In practice, few of these additional indexes are usually needed.

15.5 Referential Integrity

Referential integrity (RI) ensures that values referenced in other tables really exist. Relational databases have excellent support for referential integrity (RI) and you should use it. Many developers are wary of performance degradation, but database RI is faster than code you can write yourself. (RI logic is inside the database kernel.) Also, database RI has been extensively tested and is virtually error proof. RI guarantees that all references in a database are intact and that none are dangling.

RI declarations can have actions that specify what to do if a primary key value is updated or deleted. If you use existence-based identity, as we suggested in Chapter 6, there is no need for RI update actions; artificial identifiers are never updated, so you only need to consider RI delete actions. Most database design tools will let you specify RI actions for each association / relationship type. The SQL options are no action, restrict, cascade, set null, and set default. The appropriate choice depends on a model's meaning. For the online retail model, we set all the association foreign keys to 'no action' on delete. Thus, for example, a customer record cannot be deleted if there are corresponding address records. We set the delete action to cascade for generalizations, as the generalization levels are describing the same object.

15.6 Check Constraints

SQL also provides miscellaneous check constraints for columns and tables. We specified that *Order shippingMethod* can only have the values 'post office', 'Fed Ex', and 'UPS'. Also *OrderItem quantity* must be greater than zero, and *Product.productDiscrim* must be one of the subclass names ('Book', 'Automotive', 'Electronics', 'OtherProduct').

15.7 Views

A *view* is a SQL query that computes a database table. Views have two purposes: security and convenience. For security, a view is a different database object than the underlying table. Thus, one group of users might have access to the underlying table while another group might have access only to a view that omits some attributes. For convenience, a view can restate a table's data for easier access. For example, it is often helpful to consolidate generalization levels and see all the data for an object.

SQL databases provide robust support for reading through views. Sometimes they permit writing through views to the base table(s). We did not define any views for the online retail example.

15.8 Script to Create the Online Retail Database

Applying the rules in this chapter, Figure 15.2 creates the empty database structure for the online retail application using SQL Server.

15.9 Chapter Summary

This chapter starts with the physical data model. The first step is to revisit earlier design items (domain, data types, nulls, keys) and make sure that they are complete. You should specify referential integrity actions, as well as SQL check constraints. We applied the rules to the online retail example and prepared a SQL script to create an empty database.

```
CREATE TABLE Address (
    addressID               int identity(1,1) NOT NULL ,
    streetAddress           varchar(50)  NULL ,
    cityName                varchar(50)  NULL ,
    stateProvinceName       varchar(50)  NULL ,
    countryName             varchar(50)  NULL ,
    postalCode              varchar(20)  NULL ,
    customerID              int NOT NULL ,
CONSTRAINT pk_address PRIMARY KEY (addressID) );

CREATE INDEX i1_address ON Address (customerID);

CREATE TABLE Author (
    authorID                int identity(1,1) NOT NULL ,
    authorName              varchar(50)  NOT NULL ,
    biography               varchar(254)  NULL ,
    picture                 image  NULL ,
CONSTRAINT pk_author PRIMARY KEY (authorID) );

CREATE TABLE Automotive (
    automotiveID            int NOT NULL ,
CONSTRAINT pk_auto PRIMARY KEY (automotiveID ) );

CREATE TABLE Book (
    bookID                  int NOT NULL ,
    ISBN                    varchar(20)  NULL ,
    publishedDate           datetime  NULL ,
    format                  varchar(20)  NULL ,
    publisherName           varchar(50)  NULL ,
    language                varchar(20)  NULL ,
CONSTRAINT pk_book PRIMARY KEY (bookID) );

CREATE TABLE Book_Author (
    bookID                  int NOT NULL ,
    authorID                int NOT NULL ,
    sequenceNumber          int NOT NULL ,
CONSTRAINT pk_bk_auth PRIMARY KEY (bookID, authorID),
CONSTRAINT ak1_bk_auth UNIQUE (bookID, sequenceNumber) );

CREATE INDEX i1_bk_auth ON Book_Author (authorID);
/* A bookID index is unnecessary as it is subsumed by the PK. */
/* The index makes authorID individually accessible. */

CREATE TABLE Customer (
    customerID              int identity(1,1) NOT NULL ,
    customerName            varchar(50)  NOT NULL ,
    loginName               varchar(50)  NOT NULL ,
    encryptedPassword       varchar(50)  NOT NULL ,
CONSTRAINT pk_customer PRIMARY KEY (customerID),
CONSTRAINT ak1_customer UNIQUE (loginName) );
```

Figure 15.2 SQL Server database creation script for online retail

```
CREATE TABLE Review_Rating (
    raterID                  int NOT NULL ,
    reviewID                 int NOT NULL ,
    isHelpful                bit  NOT NULL ,
    CONSTRAINT pk_CRR PRIMARY KEY (raterID, reviewID) );

CREATE INDEX i1_CRR ON Customer_Review_rating ( reviewID );

CREATE TABLE Electronics (
    electronicsID            int NOT NULL ,
    CONSTRAINT pk_electronics PRIMARY KEY (electronicsID) );

CREATE TABLE Merchant (
    merchantID               int identity(1,1) NOT NULL ,
    merchantName             varchar(50)  NOT NULL ,
    CONSTRAINT pk_merchant PRIMARY KEY (merchantID) );

CREATE TABLE OrderTable (
    orderID                  int identity(1,1) NOT NULL ,
    orderNumber              varchar(20)  NOT NULL ,
    orderDateTime            datetime  NOT NULL ,
    shippingMethod           varchar(20)  NOT NULL
      CHECK (shippingMethod IN ('post office','Fed Ex','UPS')),
    taxAmount                money  NULL ,
    shippingHandlingAmount   money  NULL ,
    totalAmount              money  NULL ,
    shippingAddressID        int NOT NULL ,
    billingAddressID         int NOT NULL ,
    customerID               int NOT NULL ,
    CONSTRAINT pk_order PRIMARY KEY (orderID),
    CONSTRAINT ak1_order UNIQUE (orderNumber) );

CREATE INDEX i1_order ON Order ( shippingAddressID );

CREATE INDEX i2_order ON Order ( billingAddressID );

CREATE INDEX i3_order ON Order ( customerID );

CREATE TABLE OrderItem (
    orderItemID              int identity(1,1) NOT NULL ,
    quantity                 int NOT NULL CHECK (quantity > 0),
    orderID                  int NOT NULL ,
    itemNumber               varchar(20)  NOT NULL ,
    vendedProductID          int NOT NULL ,
    CONSTRAINT pk_orderitem PRIMARY KEY (orderItemID),
    CONSTRAINT ak1_orderitem UNIQUE (orderID, itemNumber) );

CREATE INDEX i1_orderitem ON OrderItem ( vendedProductID );
```

Figure 15.2 SQL Server database creation script (continued)

```
CREATE TABLE Payment (
    paymentID                int identity(1,1) NOT NULL ,
    paymentAmount            money  NULL ,
    paymentType              varchar(20)  NULL ,
    paymentDate              datetime  NOT NULL ,
    orderID                  int NOT NULL ,
    CONSTRAINT pk_payment PRIMARY KEY (paymentID) );

CREATE INDEX i1_payment ON Payment ( orderID );

CREATE TABLE Product (
    productID                int identity(1,1) NOT NULL ,
    productName              varchar(50)  NOT NULL ,
    description              varchar(254)  NULL ,
    productDiscrim           varchar(20)  NULL
      CHECK (productiscrim IN ('Book','Automotive',
      'Electronics','OtherProduct' )),
    CONSTRAINT pk_product PRIMARY KEY (productID) );

CREATE TABLE Review (
    reviewID                 int identity(1,1) NOT NULL ,
    reviewDate               datetime  NOT NULL ,
    grade                    int NOT NULL ,
    comment                  varchar(254)  NULL ,
    vendedProductID          int NOT NULL ,
    reviewerID               int NOT NULL ,
    CONSTRAINT pk_review PRIMARY KEY (reviewID) );

CREATE INDEX i1_review ON Review ( vendedProductID );

CREATE INDEX i2_review ON Review ( reviewerID );

CREATE TABLE VendedProduct (
    vendedProductID          int identity(1,1) NOT NULL ,
    price                    money  NULL ,
    condition                varchar(20)  NULL ,
    productID                int NOT NULL ,
    merchantID               int NOT NULL ,
    CONSTRAINT pk_VP PRIMARY KEY (vendedProductID) );

CREATE INDEX i1_VP ON VendedProduct ( productID );

CREATE INDEX i2_VP ON VendedProduct ( merchantID );

CREATE TABLE OtherProduct (
    otherProductID           int NOT NULL ,
    productType              varchar(20) NOT NULL ,
    CONSTRAINT pk_otherproduct PRIMARY KEY (otherProductID) );

ALTER TABLE Address ADD CONSTRAINT fk1_address
FOREIGN KEY (customerID) REFERENCES Customer
ON DELETE NO ACTION;
```

Figure 15.2 SQL Server database creation script (continued)

```
ALTER TABLE Automotive ADD CONSTRAINT fk1_automotive
FOREIGN KEY (automotiveID) REFERENCES Product
ON DELETE CASCADE;

ALTER TABLE Book ADD CONSTRAINT fk1_book
FOREIGN KEY (bookID) REFERENCES Product
ON DELETE CASCADE;

ALTER TABLE Book_Author ADD CONSTRAINT fk1_book_author
FOREIGN KEY (bookID) REFERENCES Book
ON DELETE NO ACTION;

ALTER TABLE Book_Author ADD CONSTRAINT fk2_book_author
FOREIGN KEY (authorID) REFERENCES Author
ON DELETE NO ACTION;

ALTER TABLE Review_Rating ADD CONSTRAINT fk1_rev_rating
FOREIGN KEY (raterID) REFERENCES Customer
ON DELETE NO ACTION;

ALTER TABLE Review_Rating ADD CONSTRAINT fk2_rev_rating
FOREIGN KEY (reviewID) REFERENCES Review
ON DELETE NO ACTION;

ALTER TABLE Electronics ADD CONSTRAINT fk1_electronics
FOREIGN KEY (electronicsID) REFERENCES Product
ON DELETE CASCADE;

ALTER TABLE OrderTable ADD CONSTRAINT fk1_order
FOREIGN KEY (shippingAddressID) REFERENCES Address
ON DELETE NO ACTION;

ALTER TABLE OrderTable ADD CONSTRAINT fk2_order
FOREIGN KEY (billingAddressID) REFERENCES Address
ON DELETE NO ACTION;

ALTER TABLE OrderTable ADD CONSTRAINT fk3_order
FOREIGN KEY (customerID) REFERENCES Customer
ON DELETE NO ACTION;

ALTER TABLE OrderItem ADD CONSTRAINT fk1_orderitem
FOREIGN KEY (orderID) REFERENCES OrderTable
ON DELETE NO ACTION;

ALTER TABLE OrderItem ADD CONSTRAINT fk2_orderitem
FOREIGN KEY (vendedProductID) REFERENCES VendedProduct
ON DELETE NO ACTION;

ALTER TABLE Payment ADD CONSTRAINT fk1_payment
FOREIGN KEY (orderID) REFERENCES OrderTable
ON DELETE NO ACTION;
```

Figure 15.2 SQL Server database creation script (continued)

```
ALTER TABLE Review ADD CONSTRAINT fk1_review
FOREIGN KEY (vendedProductID) REFERENCES VendedProduct
ON DELETE NO ACTION;

ALTER TABLE Review ADD CONSTRAINT fk2_review
FOREIGN KEY (reviewerID) REFERENCES Customer
ON DELETE NO ACTION;

ALTER TABLE VendedProduct ADD CONSTRAINT fk1_vendedproduct
FOREIGN KEY (productID) REFERENCES Product
ON DELETE NO ACTION;

ALTER TABLE VendedProduct ADD CONSTRAINT fk2_vendedproduct
FOREIGN KEY (merchantID) REFERENCES Merchant
ON DELETE NO ACTION;

ALTER TABLE OtherProduct ADD CONSTRAINT fk1_otherproduct
FOREIGN KEY (otherProductID) REFERENCES Product
ON DELETE CASCADE;
```

Figure 15.2 SQL Server database creation script (continued)

Bibliographic Notes

If you are using ERwin, [Burbank-2011] explains how to perform the items mentioned in this chapter. Database tools are excellent at creating an initial empty database. They are less effective at modifying a populated database. [Wikipedia] was used as a resource for some definitions.

References

[Burbank-2011] Donna Burbank and Steve Hoberman. *Data Modeling Made Simple with CA ERwin Data Modeler.* Bradley Beach, New Jersey: Technics Publications, 2011.

[Wikipedia] www.wikipedia.org

Exercises

Each exercise has a difficulty level ranging from 1 (easy) to 10 (very difficult).

15.1 (7) Consider the answer to Exercise 7.9. Add missing details and prepare a database creation script. For the purpose of this exercise, keep in mind that you can often download a database design tool for a free 30-day evaluation.

15.2 (5) Consider the answer to Exercise 5.3. Add missing details and prepare a database creation script. For the purpose of this exercise, keep in mind that you can often download a database design tool for a free 30-day evaluation.

16

Database Queries

A data model is not only useful for specifying data structure, but it can also serve as a blueprint for computation. This chapter explores the use of model traversals as an aid towards preparing SQL queries.

16.1 The Object Constraint Language (OCL)

The *Object Constraint Language (OCL)* [OMG-2012] [Warmer-2003] is a textual language that is part of the UML, and is intended for specifying constraints. The class model, by itself, can express some constraints with its data structure. The purpose of the OCL is to express additional constraints that reach beyond the class model. For example, the online retail application might require that the shipping and billing addresses for an order be found in the list of addresses for that order's customer. An OCL constraint is an expression that evaluates to true or false. The OCL is a formal, declarative language that specifies the intent of a constraint, and not its algorithmic realization.

This chapter will not comment further about using the OCL for constraints.

16.2 Using the OCL for Class Model Traversal

The OCL is useful for more than just constraints, and it can also serve as a language for class model traversals. Model traversals are important for several reasons:

- **Resolving class model defects**. Traversals help to wring out model defects. Business users pose questions against a class model and traversals are part of answering them. A traversal gap indicates that something is missing from a model. Once the flaw is apparent, you can repair and extend the model. Also you should be careful if there are multiple paths between classes. If the paths have different meanings, that is fine. However, redundant paths are usually a model defect to repair.

- **Promoting class model understanding**. Business users pose requests for functionality, often in the form of use cases. We ask them to look at the class model and see if it can satisfy their needs. This pulls them into the class model and helps them to understand it.

142

- **Specifying logic as a precursor to development**. Traversal logic is often an important aspect of functionality to be implemented. Traversal exercises a model and pulls the logic of a model into the writing of functionality.

16.3 Basic OCL Traversal Expressions

This section covers basic OCL expressions for class model traversal. By no means do we explain the full OCL language. Rather, we only discuss the portions relevant to model traversal. In the explanation, *aClassName* refers to a single object of *className*:

- **Attribute**. Traverse from an object to an attribute value. The syntax is the source object, followed by a dot, and then the attribute name. For example, the expression *anOrder.orderDateTime* takes an *Order* object and finds the value of *orderDateTime*.

Order
orderNumber (AK1.1) orderDateTime shippingMethod taxAmount shippingHandlingAmount totalAmount

order1234.orderDateTime
evaluates to Jan. 7, 2013

Figure 16.1 OCL attribute traversal.

- **Simple association**. Traverse from an object across an association to a target end. The syntax is the source object, followed by a dot, and then the target end. The target end may be indicated by an association end name or, where there is no ambiguity, a class name. In Figure 16.2, *aCustomer.Address* yields a set of addresses for a customer (the target end has "many" multiplicity). In contrast, *anOrder.shippingAddress* yields a single address (the target end has multiplicity of one).

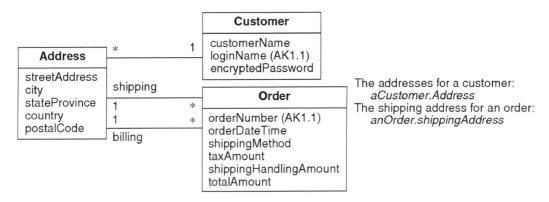

The addresses for a customer:
aCustomer.Address
The shipping address for an order:
anOrder.shippingAddress

Figure 16.2 OCL association traversal.

- **Qualified association**. Qualifiers not only improve the structure of a class model, but also improve traversal precision. You can specify a smaller and more precise collection of associated objects than without the qualifier. There are two forms of syntax.

The first ignores the qualifier and traverses the underlying association as if it were a simple association. In Figure 16.3 the expression *anOrder.OrderItem* finds the multiple *OrderItems* for an *Order*. (The multiplicity is "many" when the qualifier is not used.)

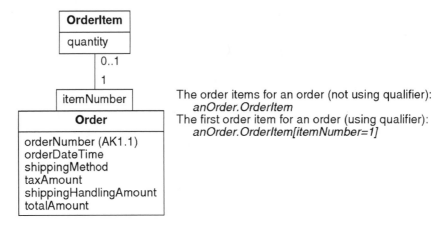

The order items for an order (not using qualifier):
   anOrder.OrderItem
The first order item for an order (using qualifier):
   anOrder.OrderItem[itemNumber=1]

Figure 16.3 OCL qualified association traversal.

The syntax for the second is the source object, followed by a dot, the target end, and finally the qualifier logic enclosed in brackets, The expression *anOrder.OrderItem[itemNumber=1]* finds the first *OrderItem* for an *Order*. Most qualified associations yield a single object.

- **Filter**. The OCL has several kinds of filters for winnowing a collection of objects, the most common of which is the *select* operation. The *select* operation applies a predicate to each element in a collection and returns the elements that satisfy the predicate. The predicate can be any expression that evaluates to true or false. Figure 16.4 uses a filter to find more specific orders for a customer. Note that *select* is preceded by -> rather than a dot; this is because *select* operates on a collection rather than individual objects.

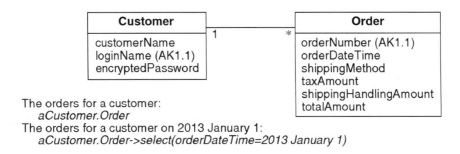

The orders for a customer:
   aCustomer.Order
The orders for a customer on 2013 January 1:
   aCustomer.Order->select(orderDateTime=2013 January 1)

Figure 16.4 OCL filtering for a set of objects

- **Association class**. There are two possible directions of traversal. Given a constituent object, you can find the multiple links of an association class. Alternatively, given a link of an association class, you can find a constituent object.

As Figure 16.5 shows, starting with a *Customer*, we can find the set of *Customer_Reviews*. The OCL requires that an association class be named so that it can be referenced. The OCL syntax is the source object, followed by a dot, and then the association class name. If we wanted to find a particular *Customer_Review* for a *Customer*, we could apply a subsequent filter.

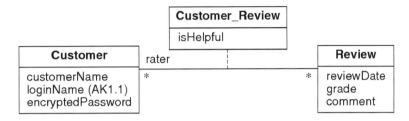

The reviews for a customer:
    aCustomer.CustomerReview
Given a Customer_Review, find the corresponding Customer:
    aCustomer_Review.Customer or *aCustomer_Review.rater*

Figure 16.5 OCL association class traversal

The second expression in Figure 16.5 starts with an association class link and traverses to an object. We can specify the desired object using the class name or the association end name. By definition a link implies one object for each role. Therefore, starting with *Customer_Review* we find a single *Customer*.

- **Generalization**. Traversal of a generalization hierarchy is implicit for the OCL. The rationale is that OCL traversal is "object-oriented" and that the multiple levels of a generalization hierarchy are all describing a single object.

16.4 Composite OCL Traversal Expressions

The real power of the OCL comes from combining constructs. For example, an OCL expression could chain together several association traversals. There could be qualifiers, filters, and operators, as well. Here are some sample expressions for the online retail model. Figure 16.6 repeats the online retail model for your convenience in following the expressions:

- Find the *Products* for an *Order*. The expression yields a bag of *Products* and we want to count each *Product* only once.
anOrder.OrderItem.VendedProduct.Product->asSet()

- Count the *Reviews* for a *Book*. The OCL operator *size* is built-in and returns the cardinality of a collection.
aBook.VendedProduct.Review->size()

- Find the total payments for a *Customer* for *Orders* in 2013. The OCL operator *sum* is built-in and tallies numeric quantities. We presume availability of the *year* function to extract the year from a date.
aCustomer.Order->select(year(orderDateTime)=2013).Payment.amount->sum()

The next sections cover subtleties that can arise from chaining together OCL expressions.

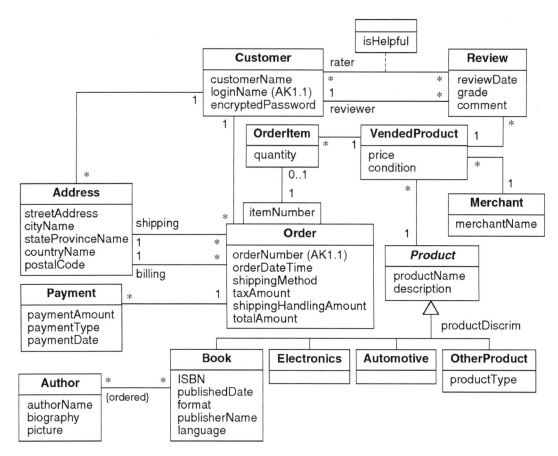

Figure 16.6 Online retail application model.

16.4.1 Objects and Object Collections

A traversal expression can start with an object or a collection of objects. Consider the following examples:

- *anOrder* is a single *Order* object.

- *anOrder.OrderItem* starts with an *Order* object and returns a collection of *OrderItem* objects.

- *anOrder.OrderItem.VendedProduct* then takes a collection of *OrderItem* objects and returns a collection of *VendedProduct* objects.

The OCL expression in the third bullet has the following meaning: (1) iterate for each *Order-Item* object in the collection, (2) for each *OrderItem* object find the associated *VendedProduct* object, and (3) return the union of the associated *VendedProduct* objects. The expression yields a bag of *VendedProducts*.

With the OCL, a traversal from an object through a single association must yield a single object or a set. However, a traversal through multiple associations can yield a bag (depending on the multiplicities), so you must be careful with OCL expressions. A *set* is a collection of elements without duplicates. A *bag* is a collection of elements with duplicates allowed.

Consider the example in Figure 16.7 of finding the *Products* for an *Order*. The OCL expression is *anOrder.OrderItem.VendedProduct.Product->asSet( )*. We start with a single *Order* object. This leads to a set of *OrderItem* objects. Looking at the model's multiplicity in Figure 16.6, each *OrderItem* has one *VendedProduct*, but each *VendedProduct* can apply to many *OrderItems*, so the additional traversal yields a bag of *VendedProduct* objects. Then, traversing from *VendedProduct* to *Product* yields a further bag.

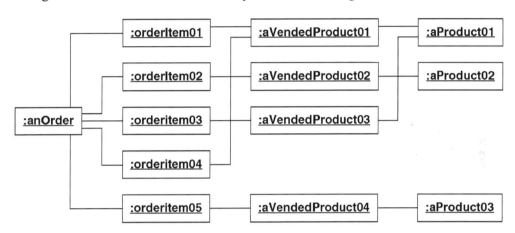

Figure 16.7 A traversal example. Traversal of multiple associations can yield a bag.

16.4.2 Dealing with Nulls

The OCL documentation does not mention null values, since it only discusses constraints. Nulls do not arise for properly phrased and valid OCL constraints. (*Null* is a special value denoting that an attribute value is unknown or not applicable.)

In contrast, the purpose in this chapter is not to specify constraints, but rather to navigate class models. Nulls can arise with model navigation. For example, a *Product* may not have any corresponding *VendedProducts*. We extend the meaning of OCL expressions to accommodate nulls—a traversal may yield a null value, and an OCL expression evaluates to null if the source object is null.

16.5 Traversing Database Tables

Model traversal is not only helpful for vetting the content of models and documenting business functionality, but is also a useful prelude to writing SQL queries.

The OCL traversal of a UML model corresponds to the traversal of database tables. However, database traversal can involve additional tables that the OCL does not show, notably many-to-many relationship types and generalization levels. You can take an OCL expression (based on a UML model) and convert it to a table traversal expression (based on an IE model). Table 16.1 revisits the expressions from Section 16.4.

Business Intent	OCL Expression	Table Traversal
Find the *Products* for an *Order*.	*anOrder.OrderItem. VendedProduct.Product ->asSet()*	*anOrder.OrderItem. VendedProduct.Product ->asSet()*
Count the *Reviews* for a *Book*.	*aBook. VendedProduct.Review->size()*	*aBook.Product. VendedProduct.Review->size()*
Find the total payments for a *Customer* for *Orders* in 2013.	*aCustomer.Order-> select(year(orderDateTime)=2013). Payment.amount->sum()*	*aCustomer.OrderTable-> select(year(orderDateTime)=2013). Payment.amount->sum()*

Table 16.1 Converting OCL expressions into table traversal expressions.

16.6 SQL Code

The final step is to take a table traversal expression and write the corresponding SQL code. Table traversals become SQL joins. Ordinary indexes and clustered indexes can speed up these joins. The multiplicity of the relationship type (mandatory or optional) determines if there is an inner join or outer join. None of the online retail application queries require outer joins, but Exercise 16.3 does. Table 16.2 converts table traversal expressions into SQL code.

Table Traversal	SQL Code
anOrder.OrderItem. VendedProduct.Product- >asSet()	SELECT DISTINCT P.productID, P.productName FROM OrderTable O INNER JOIN OrderItem OI ON O.orderID = OI.orderID INNER JOIN VendedProduct VP ON OI.vendedProductID = VP.vendedProductID INNER JOIN Product P ON VP.productID = P.productID;

aBook.Product. VendedProduct.Review->size()	SELECT COUNT(*)
	FROM Book B
	INNER JOIN Product P ON B.bookID = P.productID
	INNER JOIN VendedProduct VP
	  ON P.productID = VP.productID
	INNER JOIN Review R
	  ON VP.vendedProductID = R.vendedProductID;

aCustomer.OrderTable-> select(year(orderDateTime)=2013). Payment.amount->sum()	SELECT SUM (P.amount) FROM Customer C INNER JOIN OrderTable O ON C.customerID = O.customerID INNER JOIN Payment P ON O.orderID = P.orderID WHERE year(O.orderDateTime) = '2013';

Table 16.2 Converting table traversal expressions into SQL code.

16.7 Chapter Summary

A data model is not only useful for specifying data structure, but it can also serve as a blueprint for computation. The Object Constraint Language (OCL) is a textual language that is part of the UML and is intended for specifying constraints. More important for this chapter, the OCL can also serve as a language for specifying model traversals. We have shown how to take traversal expressions based on a UML model and convert them to table traversals based on an IE model. The table traversals then become the basis for writing SQL code.

Bibliographic Notes

[Celko-2010] is an excellent book that covers fine points of SQL and advanced SQL queries. Advanced SQL queries can be difficult to write, but can save days of programming effort and debugging. [OMG-2012] has the formal OMG OCL specification. [Warmer-2003] provides additional OCL explanation.

References

[Celko-2010] Joe Celko. *SQL for Smarties, Fourth Edition: Advanced SQL Programming*. New York: Morgan Kaufmann, 2010.

[OMG-2012] http://www.omg.org/spec/OCL/2.3.1/

[Warmer-2003] Jos Warmer and Anneke Kleppe. *The Object Constraint Language: Getting Your Models Ready for MDA (2nd Edition)*. Reading, Massachusetts: Addison-Wesley, 2003.

Exercises

Each exercise has a difficulty level ranging from 1 (easy) to 10 (very difficult).

16.1 (5) Prepare a database traversal expression and SQL code for the OCL expression *aProduct.VendedProduct.Review.rater->asSet()*. This OCL expression is based on the model in Figure 2.1 and Figure 2.2.

16.2 (8) Consider the answer to Exercise 7.9. Write an OCL expression, a database traversal expression, and SQL code for each of the following business inquiries:
a. For what course names is a student registered in a specified semester?
b. What is the average grade for a student in courses for their major department?

16.3 (7) Consider the answer to Exercise 7.10. Return data for the *Transactions* for a *CheckingAccount* including data about the *Statement*, if the *Transaction* has been listed on one. Write an OCL expression, a database traversal expression, and SQL code.

Test 4

Database Design

1. When you prepare UML and IE models, which of the following is the better approach? Explain your answer.
   a. Just directly specify data types and omit domains.
   b. Specify attributes in terms of domains and separately specify the data type for each domain.

2. For which of the following should you not define database indexes? Explain your answer.
   a. For combinations of attributes that are often accessed.
   b. For each foreign key that is not subsumed by a primary key or alternate key constraint.
   c. For primary and alternate keys.
   d. None of the above.

3. Which of the following are correct statements. Explain your answer.
   a. You should avoid using referential integrity because of the overhead cost.
   b. Use referential integrity to avoid dangling references to data.
   c. Forego referential integrity because you can use database triggers instead.
   d. All of the above.

4. Traversal to an association end with zero or one multiplicity always results in an outer join. Explain your answer.
   a. True
   b. False

5. Why is it important to also think in terms of computation when evaluating a data model. Explain your answer.
   a. Business queries can help uncover flaws in a data model.
   b. Business queries help users grasp the significance of a model and relate it to their needs.
   c. Business queries help to specify logic that is needed in building applications.
   d. All of the above.

Answers

Chapter 3

Some of the exercises have multiple correct answers.

3.1 Classes include league, team, game, inning, player, position, plate appearance, and umpire.

3.2 Classes include health spa, room, therapist, treatment, customer, and appointment. There are additional subtle classes such as work session (contiguous hours of work for a therapist on a particular day, such as 9 AM to 5 PM on March 14, 2010) and payment.

3.3 Classes include Auction, AuctionItem, Bid, Bidder, Feedback, ItemCategory, PaymentMethod, Reply, and Seller.

3.4 Classes include Menu, MenuItem, Restaurant, ItemCategory (Appetizer, Salad, Entree, Beverage), and EatingTime (breakfast, lunch, dinner).

3.5 Here is a determination as class or attribute and a brief explanation for each decision.

- network — class. A network can have descriptive data (name, logo).
- program — class. A program can have descriptive data.
- listing — class.
- program name — attribute. Describes a program.
- new or repeat — attribute with an enumeration domain. Describes a listing.
- listing date — attribute. Describes a listing.
- start time — attribute. Describes a listing.
- duration — attribute. Describes a program (such as a 108 minute movie) as well as a listing (120 minutes including commercials).
- program category — either a class or an attribute, depending on the modeler's perspective. Refers to a program. If it is a class, program category can have a name and description. If it is an attribute, it is enumerated and can be movies, sports, family, or news.
- synopsis — attribute. Describes a program.
- year released — attribute. Describes a program.
- director — class. Pertains to a person and can have descriptive data.
- actor/actress — class. Pertains to a person and can have descriptive data.
- carrier — class. A carrier can have descriptive data.

- channel — attribute. Pertains to a listing.
- rating — class. A rating can have descriptive data, such as a name, code, and description.
- rating reason — class. This is a lightweight class, but it has at least two attributes (code and description).

3.6   Figure A3.1 shows the auto dealer model with attributes added.

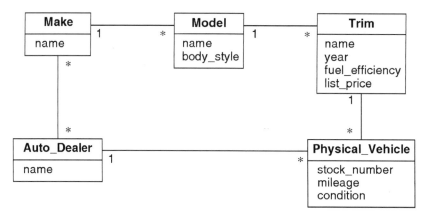

Figure A3.1 Auto dealer model with attributes

3.7   Figure A3.2 shows the course model with attributes added. We presume that a *Department* issues a new *ListedCourse* catalog each year. Some courses can be shared across *Departments*, but we presume that each *ListedCourse* is per *Department* as the code and description can vary.

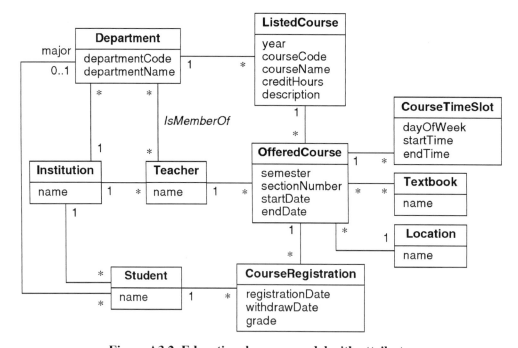

Figure A3.2 Educational course model with attributes

Note that a *CourseTimeSlot* belongs to a single *OfferedCourse*. This specificity makes it easier to maintain the database as updates occur. This model representation is not a limitation as one *CourseTimeSlot* record from 8-9 AM on Monday can belong to an *OfferedCourse* and another *CourseTimeSlot* record also from 8-9 AM on Monday can belong to a different *Offered-Course*.

3.8   Figure A3.3 shows the elaborated model. Here are definitions of the operations:

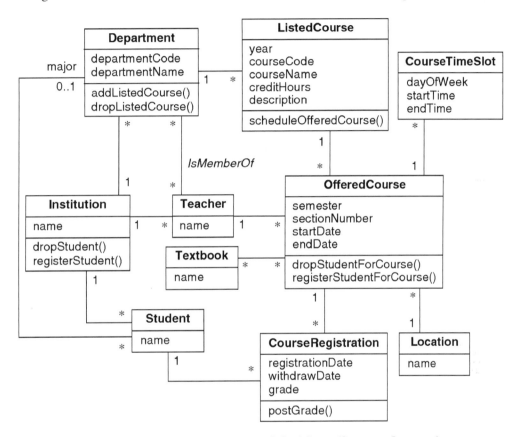

Figure A3.3 Educational course model with attributes and operations

- **addListedCourse** — add a new *ListedCourse* for a *Department*. It is an error if the *Listed-Course code* or *name* already exists for the *Department*.
- **dropListedCourse** — delete a *ListedCourse* for a *Department*. It is an error if the *Listed-Course code* or *name* does not exist for the *Department*. It is an error if the *ListedCourse* has any *OfferedCourses*. (Otherwise there could be dangling references.) It would probably be a good idea to add attributes *effectiveDate* and *expirationDate* for *ListedCourse*. (Chapter 6 discusses historical data and use of effective and expiration dates.)
- **dropStudent** — delete a *Student* for an *Institution*. It is an error if the *Student* has any *CourseRegistrations*.
- **dropStudentForCourse** — delete the *CourseRegistration* of a *Student* for an *Offered-Course*. It is an error if the *CourseRegistration* does not exist. It is also an error if the *Course-Registration* has a *grade* other than NULL. This operation could be assigned to *Student* instead of *OfferedCourse*.

- **postGrade** — set the value of the *grade* for a *CourseRegistration*. It is an error if the *Course-Registration* does not exist.

- **registerStudent** — add a new *Student* for an *Institution*. The model would need to be extended to have some way of uniquely identifying each *Student*. It is an error if the *Student* is already in the database and associated with the *Institution*.

- **registerStudentForCourse** — add a *CourseRegistration* for a *Student* and *OfferedCourse*. It is an error if the *Student* is already registered for the *OfferedCourse*. This operation could be assigned to *Student* instead of *OfferedCourse*.

- **scheduleOfferedCourse** — create an *OfferedCourse* for a *ListedCourse* with the specified *semester*, *sectionNumber*, *startDate*, *endDate*, *CourseTimeSlots*, *Textbooks*, *Location*, and *Teacher*. It is an error if the *semester* and *sectionNumber* already exist for the *ListedCourse*. Also check for schedule conflicts for the *Teacher* and *Location* (if a physical *Location*).

3.9   Here are the domains for the attributes.

- body_style: body_style
- condition: condition
- fuel_efficiency: number
- list_price: money
- mileage: number
- name: name
- stock_number: stock_number
- year: year

3.10   Here is the data dictionary.

- **CourseRegistration**. The registration of a *Student* for an *OfferedCourse*. There can be multiple registrations of a *Student* for an *OfferedCourse* if there is a registration, withdrawal, and then another registration, although it seldom occurs.

- **CourseTimeSlot**. A *dayOfWeek*, *startTime*, and *endTime* for an *OfferedCourse*. Example: Wednesday from 9 AM to 10 AM. An *OfferedCourse* will usually have several *Course-TimeSlots* such as Monday, Wednesday, and Friday from 9–10 AM.

- **Department**. A portion of an institution dedicated to a discipline. A department offers one or more series of *ListedCourses* that can lead to a degree. Examples: accounting, sociology, and computer engineering.

- **Institution**. An organization that provides courses. Covers universities and technical schools, as well as online teaching.

- **ListedCourse**. A course as described in a catalog for a degree program of a *Department*.

- **Location**. The campus building and room where an *OfferedCourse* is held or a URL (for an online *OfferedCourse*).

- **OfferedCourse**. A *ListedCourse* taught as a particular section in a year, semester, and time slots by a *Teacher*.

- **Student**. Someone who takes courses towards a degree from a *Department* of an *Institution*.

- **Teacher**. A member of one or more *Departments* who can teach *OfferedCourses*. *Teachers* can be full time or part time, as well as members of the faculty or adjunct.

- **Textbook**. A book that is assigned for an *OfferedCourse*. Textbooks can vary for the *Offered-Courses* of a *ListedCourse* from year to year and according to *Teacher* preferences.

Chapter 4

Some of the exercises have multiple correct answers.

4.1   Figure A4.1 shows a UML model for the baseball example. Note the following details about the model.

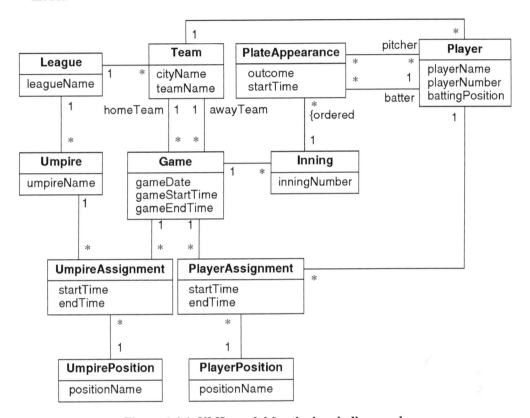

Figure A4.1 UML model for the baseball example

- Both *gameDate* and *gameStartTime* are needed to cover double headers (two games played on the same day).
- Possible *battingPositions* are left, right, and switch.
- The *playerNumber* (the number on the uniform) can change over time. This model stores the current number.
- Some *PlayerPositions* are pitcher, catcher, and first base.
- Some *outcomes* are walk, single, error, and hit by pitch.
- Normally a *PlateAppearance* is for one pitcher, but it can be for multiple pitchers (such as if there is an injury or a pitcher is relieved).
- A player may go back and forth to the same position. Example: a player starts in left field, moves to first base, then moves back to left field.
- The *PlateAppearances* for an *Inning* are ordered. Chapter 7 discusses ordering.

4.2   Figure A4.2 shows an IE model for the baseball example. We prefer to assign each entity type its own ID and minimize use of dependent entity types.

4.3   Figure A4.3 shows the UML model for the health spa example.

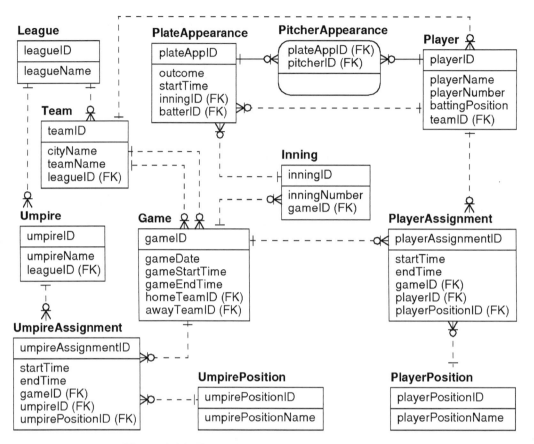

Figure A4.2 IE model for the baseball example

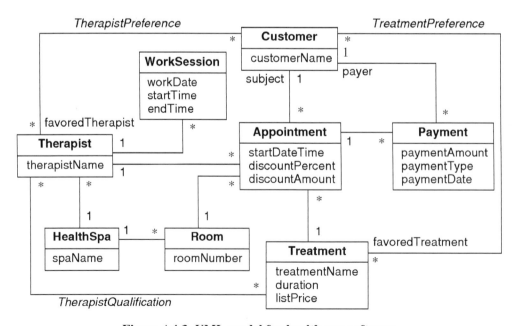

Figure A4.3 UML model for health spa software

4.4 Figure A4.4 shows the UML model for the online auction problem. The buyer of an *AuctionItem* is the *Customer* with the highest *Bid.maxPrice*. The model omits *Auction,* as some online auction sites just have items starting at various times and have no specific notion of an *Auction.*

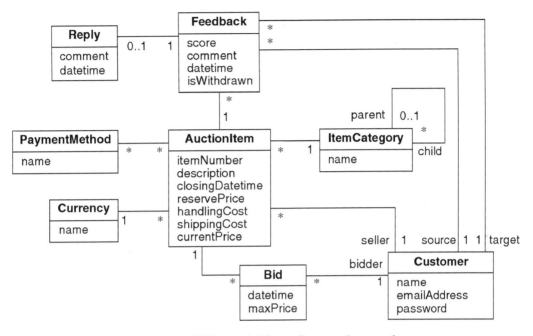

Figure A4.4 UML model for online auction auctions

4.5 Figure A4.5 shows a UML model for Netflix movie rentals. Note that a *Customer* may request the same movie more than once, so a many-to-many association between *Movie* and *Customer* is not correct, hence the class *MovieRequest*. The collection of *MovieRequests* that have not been sent comprise the "movie request list". As Chapter 7 explains, we could add an attribute to capture each individual *Customer* rating with a many-to-many association class between *Movie* and *Customer*. Most *Customers* will have a specified *Address* for receiving movie discs.

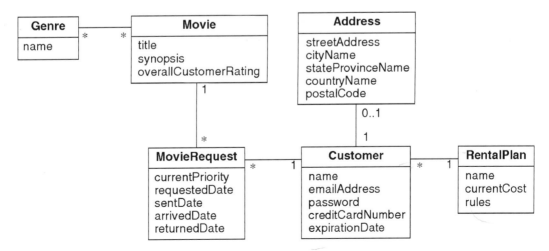

Figure A4.5 UML model for Netflix

4.6   Figure A4.6 shows the improved timesheet model. We presume that a *Project* can have more
than three categories and introduced a many-to-many association.

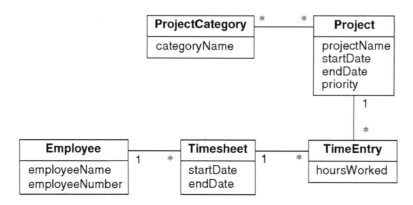

Figure A4.6 Improved timesheet model

4.7   Figure A4.7 adds association names to Figure 2.1.

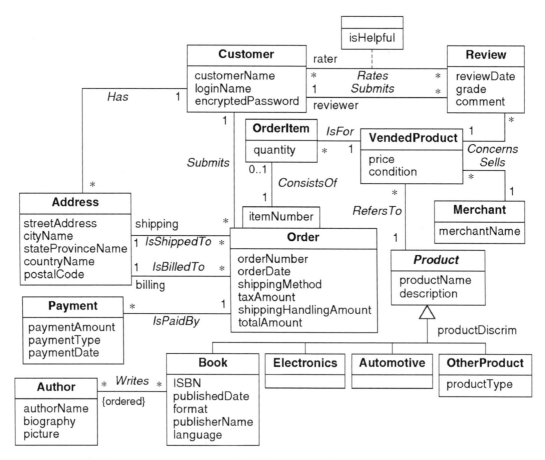

Figure A4.7 Online retail UML model with association names

4.8   Figure A4.8 adds directed relationship type names to Figure 2.2.

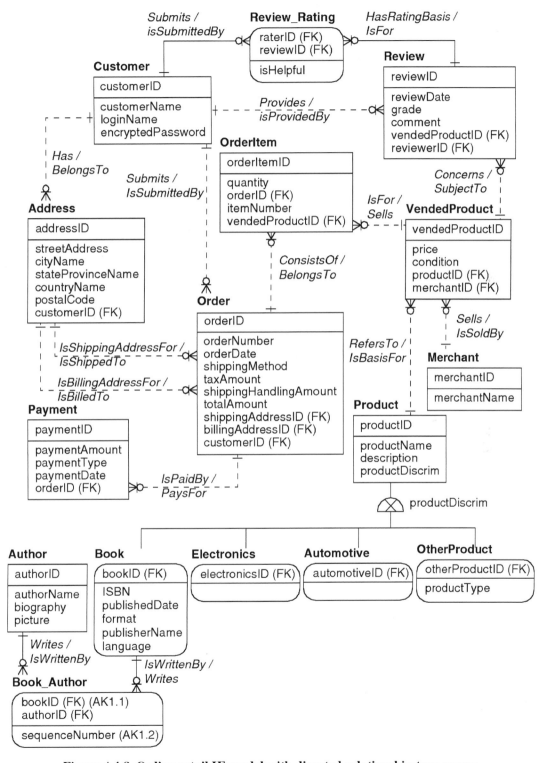

Figure A4.8 Online retail IE model with directed relationship type names

4.9   Figure A4.9 shows the LinkedIn model. The links between members establish connectivity. A *Link* connects exactly two *Members*. You could have modeled this as a *Link* connects many *Members*.

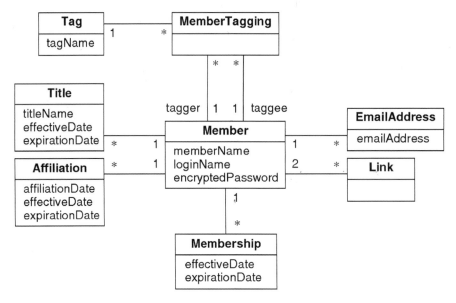

Figure A4.9 UML model for LinkedIn

4.10   Figure A4.10 shows the TV listing model with multiplicity.

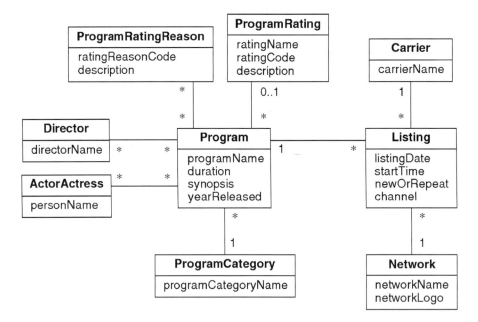

Figure A4.10 UML model for TV listings

4.11 Figure A4.11 shows the auto insurance model with multiplicity. An *Insured* person has multiple *AutoInsuranceCards* over time (though there should be only one card at a time, a constraint which the model does not enforce). An *InsurancePolicy* concerns one *PhysicalVehicle*. A *PhysicalVehicle* can have multiple *InsurancePolicies*, such as when there is a change of *CoverageItems*.

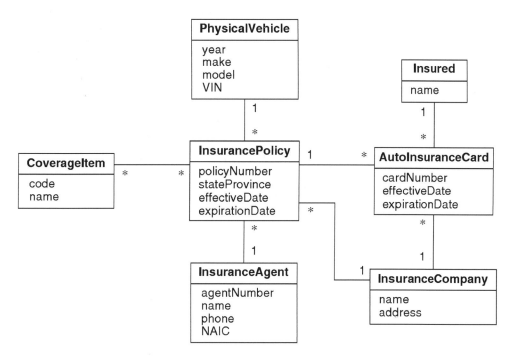

Figure A4.11 UML model for auto insurance

4.12 Figure A4.12 shows the UML model for U.S. customs declarations.

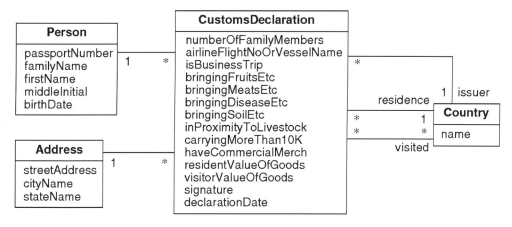

Figure A4.12 UML model for U.S. customs declarations

Chapter 5

Some of the exercises have multiple correct answers.

5.1 Not really.

UmpirePositions are distinct from PlayerPositions so there is no reason to generalize them. For example, PlayerPositions include catcher, pitcher, first base, short stop, and center fielder. UmpirePositions include home plate umpire, first base umpire, and second base umpire. There is no umpire at the pitcher, short stop, or center field positions.

Similarly, there is no reason to generalize Umpire and Player. Umpires are managed by the League office. In contrast, Players belong to a Team.

5.2 Figure A5.1 shows the extended spa model with different kinds of payments. We renamed paymentType to paymentDiscriminator.

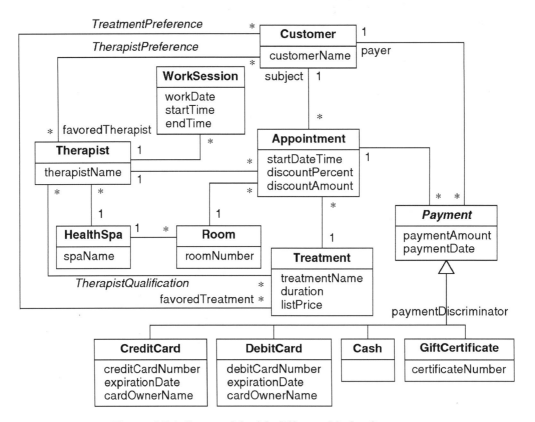

Figure A5.1 Spa model with different kinds of payments

5.3 Figure A5.2 shows the improved model. A FoodProduct has many Ingredients, each of which can be a lesser FoodProduct or a BaseIngredient.

5.4 Figure A5.3 shows the UML model.

5.5 Figure A5.4 shows the simpler UML model with generalization.

5.6 Figure A5.5 shows the generalization hierarchy. The associations in the model were implied by the requirements, but were not requested.

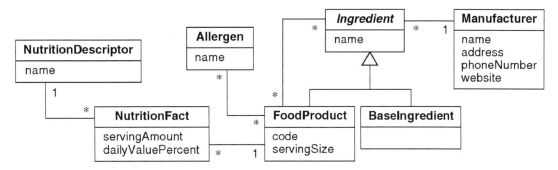

Figure A5.2 Improved model for food products

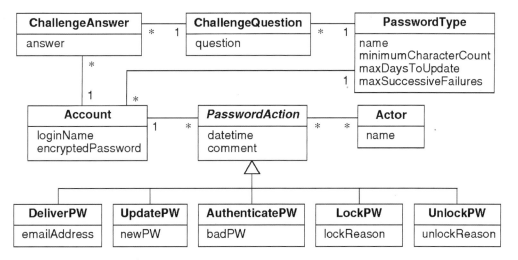

Figure A5.3 UML model for checking accounts

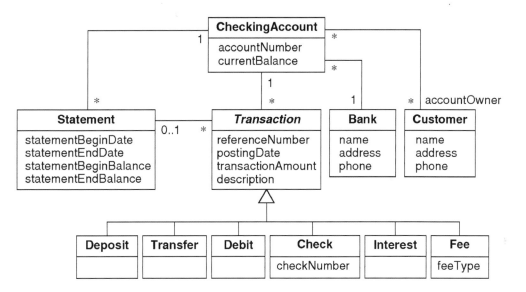

Figure A5.4 Restructured UML model using generalization

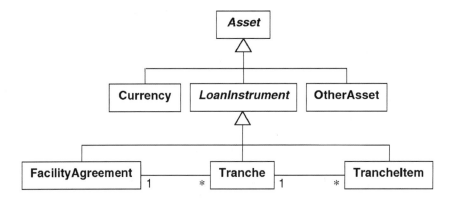

Figure A5.5 UML generalization hierarchy for syndicated loans

5.7   There are two superclasses in Figure A5.5. *Asset* is obviously abstract, given that it has the *OtherAsset* subclass. *LoanInstrument* is also abstract, although that is not clear from the requirements statement.

5.8   Figure A5.6 shows an IE diagram that corresponds to Figure A5.5.

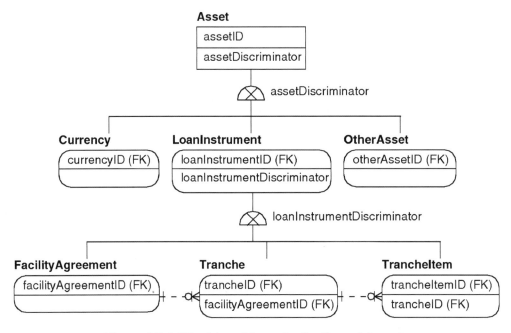

Figure A5.6 IE subtype hierarchy for financial assets

5.9   Figure A5.7 restates Figure A5.6 to forego subtype renaming of foreign key references to the supertype. This is the diagram that ERwin displays. Note the ambiguity in the relationship types from *TrancheItem* to *Tranche* and from *Tranche* to *FacilityAgreement*. For example, there is one *Tranche.assetID* that refers to *LoanInstrument* and another *Tranche.assetID* that refers to *FacilityAgreement*. You can avoid such confusion if you make each object ID name correspond to its class name.

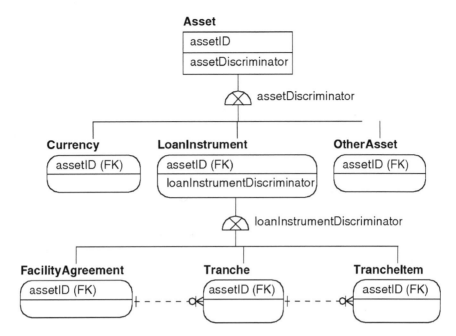

Figure A5.7 IE hierarchy for financial assets without subtype renaming

Test 1

Congratulations if you get eight or more answers correct. Such a high score demonstrates that you understand the material well. If you score lower, you should go back and review the text and exercises.

Keep in mind that the test covers only some of the material in Part 1.

1. c   For a wrong answer, see Section 4.5.

2. a   But it is not especially useful. One purpose of domains is to specify data types that are reusable across attributes.

For a wrong answer, see Section 3.4.

3. a   The top model is clearly better. It is not helpful to restrict a person arbitrarily to a limit of three employers. The meaning of first, second, and third employer is unclear. Furthermore, it could be awkward updating data, as a person changes employers. The addition of a fourth employer could cause the oldest employer to be dropped and a ripple update from first to second to third.

For a wrong answer, revisit Chapter 4. It is important to understand many-to-many associations.

4. a   A person's birthdate does not change, whereas their age changes over the years. If an application needs a person's age, it would be better to compute it from birthdate. This is a simple example of derived data that Chapter 6 covers in more detail.

5. a   Every item in the sample data is covered by the model. This is a question about the meaning of a model.

For a wrong answer, revisit Chapter 3 and Chapter 4.

6. a   This is a valid UML model. An end name must not clash with any other attribute or end name of the origination class. There is no clash in this model.

For a wrong answer, see Section 4.3.

7. b   An identifying relationship type must connect to a dependent entity type. *D* should be a rounded box.

For a wrong answer, see Section 4.1.

8. b   It makes no sense for generalization to have a cycle.

For a wrong answer, revisit Chapter 5.

9. a   Generalization structures the description of occurrences. The models differ in how the description is organized, but store the same objects in either case.

For a wrong answer, revisit Chapter 5.

10. b   The right model is clearly better for building software.

The left model has separate classes for *IndividualContributor*, *Supervisor*, and *Manager*. Each of the classes would repeat common data such as phone numbers and addresses. What happens when an *IndividualContributor* is promoted to a *Supervisor*? Is the record moved? Is it copied? The right model has a single record for a *Person* and there is no ambiguity about where to store data.

The left model is also inflexible. For example, we must add the *Director* class to permit bosses for *Managers*. The right model requires no such addition. The right model has no artificial limit on the number of levels of the hierarchy.

The right model is more abstract, and as a consequence, more lax with constraints. For example, the right model would permit nonsensical data where a *Manager* reports to an *IndividualContributor*. Also the right model is less understandable to end users.

In practice, we build software using the right model. We use the left model to demonstrate examples for users and to provide data for populating the right model.

This question stresses the importance of model abstraction, which we emphasize throughout the book.

Chapter 6

Some of the exercises have multiple correct answers.

6.1 Figure A6.1 shows the auto dealer model with alternate keys added.

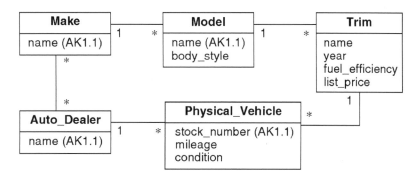

Figure A6.1 Auto dealer model with attributes and alternate keys

6.2 Figure A6.2 shows an IE auto dealer model with existence-based identity.

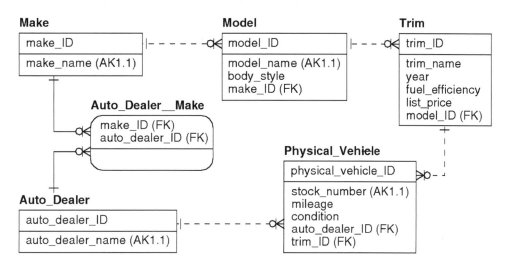

Figure A6.2 Auto dealer model with existence-based identity

6.3 Figure A6.3 shows an IE auto dealer model with value-based identity, where possible.

6.4 If *userID* was the primary key of *Customer*, tables that refer to *Customer* would contain *userID* as a foreign key. This would make it awkward if a customer were to change their *userID* -- a change to *userID* would ripple throughout the database. It is highly likely that online auction software has used object identity for customer — an arbitrary number for each customer. The object identifier is hidden from the user interface and is used internally for foreign key references to *Customer*. The *userID* then is just an ordinary attribute (that also happens to be unique) and can be freely edited by a customer with little effect on database data and performance.

We've seen some Web sites that appear to have *Customer* email address as the primary key. These Web sites typically won't let a *Customer* change their email address once the account is created. Such a restriction is annoying and unnecessary.

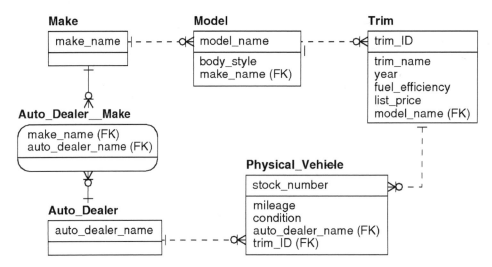

Figure A6.3 Auto dealer model with value-based identity where possible

6.5   Figure A6.4 revises an excerpt of Figure 2.1. A *Product* can go off the market, such as when a *Product* is discontinued. A *VendedProduct* can go off the market, such as when a *Merchant* no longer sells a *Product*.

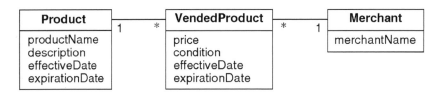

Figure A6.4 Tracking historical data for *Product* and *VendedProduct*

6.6   Figure A6.5 revises a portion of the educational course model. The model can track when *Departments* are started and terminated for an *Institution*.

Note that Figure A6.5 permits a *Teacher* to join a *Department*, leave the *Department*, and then join the *Department* again, which is permissible behavior.

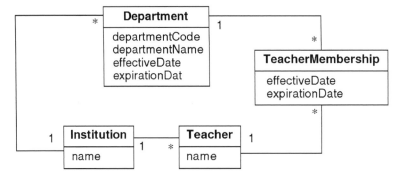

Figure A6.5 Educational course model with added history

6.7 In the top model an *Address* always belongs to a single *Customer*. The bottom model has no such restriction — an *Address* record could have multiple *AddressHistory* records referring to different *Customers*.

6.8 The models in Figure A6.6 correspond to Figure E6.1 and only store current data.

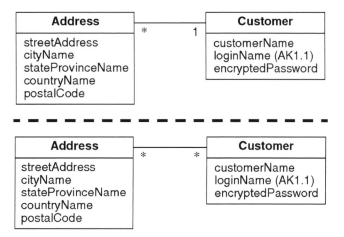

Figure A6.6 Alternative models for current address data

6.9 Figure A6.7 shows the revised model. A reservation may not have a rental (such as if the customer is a no-show). If a rental is booked on the spot, we regard it as having a reservation created at that time. Thus, the association from reservation to customer suffices. A reservation is for a rate class; at the time of rental an actual vehicle is assigned. The pickup location must be that specified by the reservation. The drop-off can change if the customer happens to return the vehicle to a different location. Payment can be made at the time of reservation or rental.

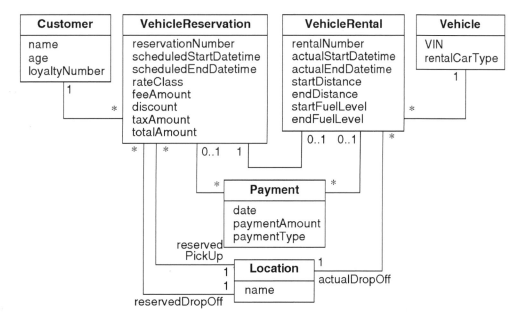

Figure A6.7 Revised model for vehicle rental data

6.10   Figure A6.8 revises the model. Given that new licenses are being issued each day and old licenses are continually expiring, the database would most likely store both past and present licenses. Therefore, the database structure must allow multiple licenses for a person. Note that the database cannot reasonably enforce that a person has no more than one active license. Business processes would need to deal with the situation where more than one active license is found.

You could have *signature* and *photo* as attributes of *Person*, but it is better to assign them to *DriversLicense*, as the *signature* and *photo* is for the particular *DriversLicense*.

There is an *issuing StateProvince* and an *Address StateProvince*. We are not sure if they always must match.

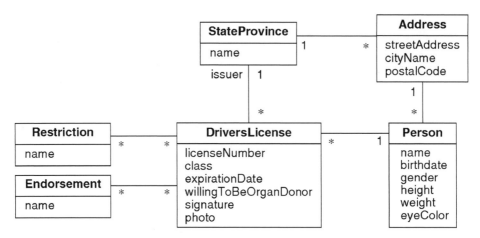

Figure A6.8   Improved driver's license model

6.11   *Person* is the fundamental name of the class. *Driver* is really an association end name. If the model is extended, then *Person* may appear in different ways (such as the agent providing insurance, the police officer writing a ticket, and the clerk in the license office who handles renewal paperwork). If these name spaces are disjoint, then *Person* could be replaced by *Driver*, *InsuranceAgent*, *PoliceOfficer*, and so forth. However, the *Person* class would be needed if it was important to find all police officers with major traffic tickets (the same person is a driver in some records and a police officer in others).

Chapter 7

Some of the exercises have multiple correct answers.

7.1   The top model permits the same *Person* to be both a *director* and an *actor* for the same *Program*. The lower model only permits a *Person* to be a *director* or *actor* for a *Program*. Since there are programs where the same person both acts and directs, the top model is the better model.

7.2   Figure A7.1 shows IE models for Figure E7.1.

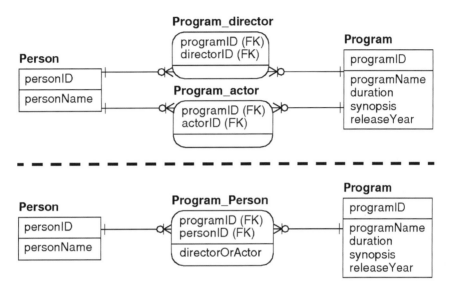

Figure A7.1 Alternative IE models excerpts for TV programs

7.3   Figure A7.2 shows the UML model. The *ItemPrice* association class allows the price for an item to vary for breakfast, lunch, or dinner, as well as over time. *EatingTimes* include breakfast, lunch, dinner, and late night. The model could be useful for a restaurant Web site.

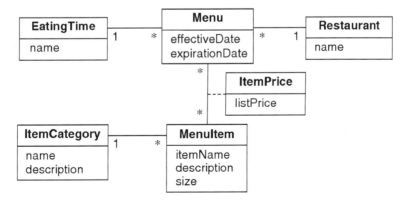

Figure A7.2 Restaurant menu UML model

7.4   Figure A7.3 shows the Netflix UML model with individual ratings as an association class.

7.5   Add *{ordered}* to the model. A *FoodProduct* has an ordered list of *Ingredients*.

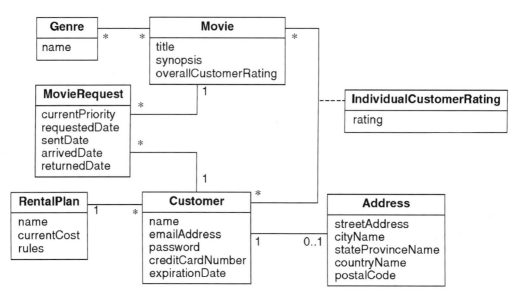

Figure A7.3 UML model for Netflix movie rentals

7.6 The model with the qualifier is correct, but there doesn't seem to be much purpose. The qualifier reduces the multiplicity of the target listings, but it is still a collection. In general, qualifiers are only worthwhile if they reduce multiplicity from many to one.

7.7 Figure E7.3 is clearly better than Figure E7.2. At least the qualifiers reduce multiplicity from many to one. It's not clear if the model in Figure A4.10 or Figure E7.3 is best, because the use of three qualifiers is cumbersome.

7.8 Figure A7.4 shows the IE model.

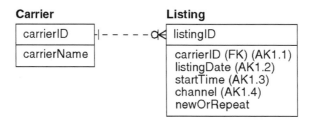

Figure A7.4 IE counterpart to UML model with multiple qualifiers

7.9 Figure A7.5 shows the course model with qualifiers.

7.10 Figure A7.6 shows the checking account model with qualifiers.

7.11 Figure A7.7 shows the IE model with existence-based identity. Figure A7.8 shows the IE model with value-based identity. Note that *countryID* + *spAbbrev* also is an alternate key, even though the UML model does not specify it.

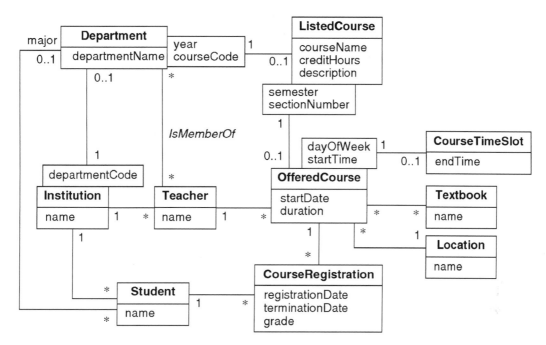

Figure A7.5 Educational course model with qualifiers

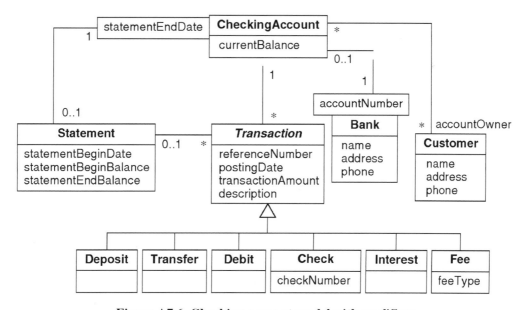

Figure A7.6 Checking account model with qualifiers

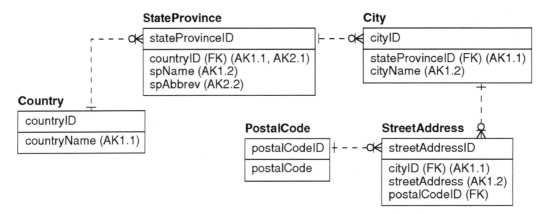

Figure A7.7 Cascaded qualifiers with existence-based identity

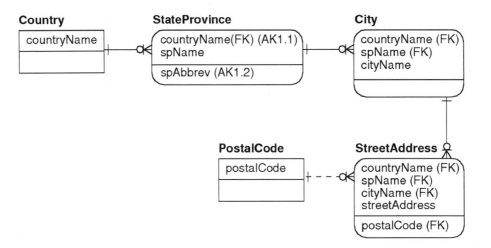

Figure A7.8 Cascaded qualifiers with value-based identity

Chapter 8

Some of the exercises have multiple correct answers.

8.1   All three model excerpts are correct and are viable options.

Exclusive-or associations infrequently occur; they can be awkward to explain and difficult to enforce with a database.

The middle model avoids the exclusive-or association by defining a superclass for *Program* and *Episode*. This makes the model larger. Also the database design must still cope with exclusive-or (but now from the generalization). If there were other generalization bases for *Program* and/or *Episode*, the generalization to *ListingItem* would lead to multiple inheritance, which is problematic for data models.

A third option is for all programs to have episodes. The degenerate case is one episode for a program. We prefer this option. The model is small in size and straightforward for development.

8.2   Figure A8.1 adds the *Watch* class that is associated to *AuctionItem* and *Customer*. No other changes are necessary. Note that whether an *AuctionItem* is active can be derived by comparing the current time with the closing time of the *AuctionItem*.

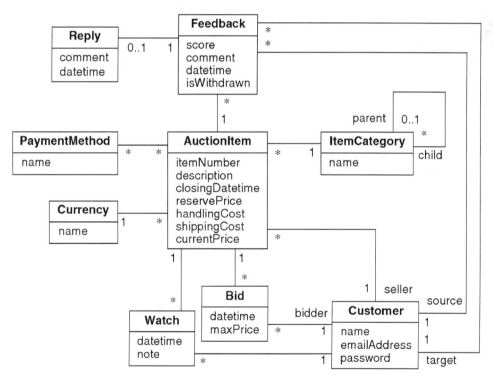

Figure A8.1 Online auction model with a *Watch* class

8.3   The model in Figure A8.2 generalizes *Watch* and *Bid*.

8.4   Here are the populated tables.

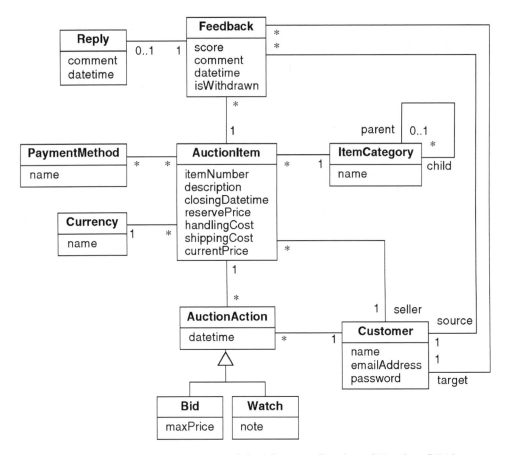

Figure A8.2 Online auction model with generalization of *Watch* and *Bid*

ProductType table	
productTypeID	**typeName**
1	Product
2	Book
3	Electronics
4	Automotive
5	OtherProduct
6	Computer

ProductType table (continued)	
productTypeID	**typeName**
7	OtherElectronics
8	Desktop
9	Laptop
10	Netbook
11	Tablet
12	OtherComputer

ProductAttribute table

product AttributeID	attribute Name	product TypeID
1	productName	1
2	description	1
3	ISBN	2
4	publishedDate	2
5	format	2
6	publisherName	2
7	language	2
8	productType	5
11	electronicsType	7
12	operatingSystem	9

ProductAttribute table (continued)

product AttributeID	attribute Name	product TypeID
13	displaySize	9
14	processorType	9
15	ramSize	9
16	hardDriveSize	9
17	graphics Processor	9
18	flashSize	9
19	brand	9
20	cpuSpeed	9
21	computerType	12

ProductGeneralization table

product GeneralizationID	discriminator	categoryID
1	productDiscrim	1
2	electronicsDiscrim	3
3	computerDiscrim	6

ProductGeneralization_subcategory table

product GeneralizationID	subcategory ID
1	2
1	3
1	4
1	5
2	6
2	7

ProductGeneralization_subcategory table (continued)

product GeneralizationID	subcategory ID
3	8
3	9
3	10
3	11
3	12

Chapter 9

Some of the exercises have multiple correct answers.

9.1   Figure A9.1 shows the extended model that supports multiple locations. A *HealthSpa* has many *Locations* and a *Location* has many *Rooms*. A *WorkSession* is for a particular *Location*.

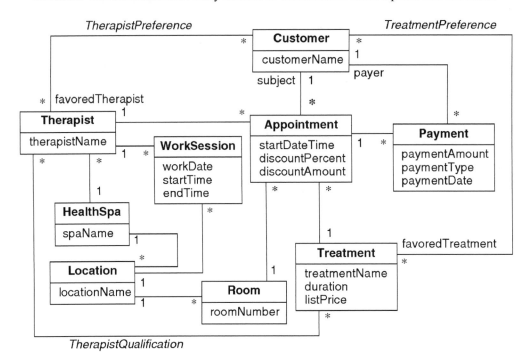

Figure A9.1 Health spa model with multiple locations

9.2   Figure A9.2 through Figure A9.4 show the model for each package.

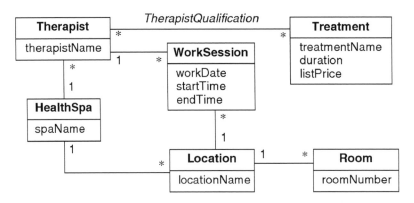

Figure A9.2 Location package for the health spa model with multiple locations

9.3   Figure A9.5 shows the model of schedules for a sporting league with seat pricing data. The possible values for *gameType* are pre-season, regular season, and post-season. The *ActualPrice* that a *Customer* pays for a *Seat* can differ from the *ListPrice* for its *SeatCategory*.

Figure A9.3 Customer package for the health spa model with multiple locations

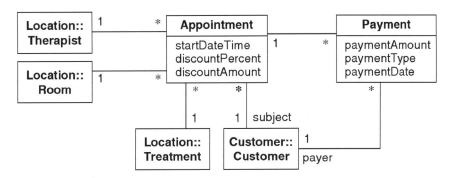

Figure A9.4 Appointment package for the health spa model with multiple locations

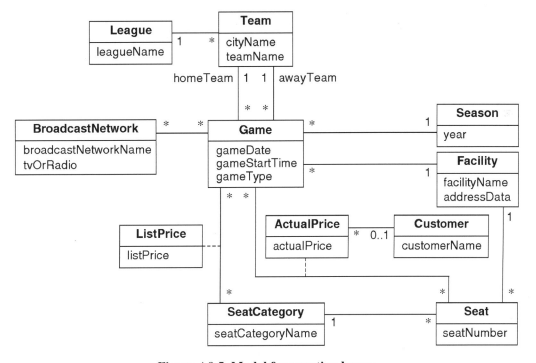

Figure A9.5 Model for sporting league

9.4 It's clear that the model can be divided into two packages — one focusing on the schedule (Figure A9.6) and the other on pricing (Figure A9.7).

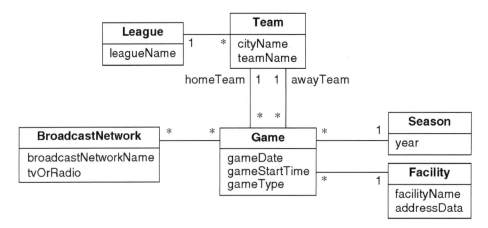

Figure A9.6 Schedule package for the sporting league model

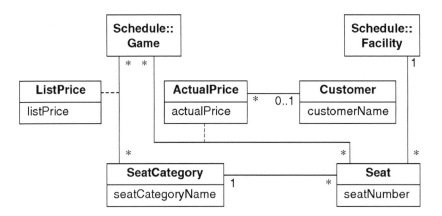

Figure A9.7 Price package for sporting league model

Chapter 10

Some of the exercises have multiple correct answers.

10.1 The combination of *ConferenceYear* and *ConferenceSeries* in Figure E10.1 violates second normal form. Also the *emailAddress* is transitively dependent on the chair person, who in turn, depends on the *ConferenceYear*, violating third normal form. The model in Figure A10.1 is in third normal form.

Figure A10.1 Revised conference model in third normal form

10.2 In the original model, *toRecipients* and *ccRecipients* violate first normal form as they are repeating groups. The original model also violates third normal form, as the email password depends on the account name which, in turn, can vary by email message (a transitive dependency). The model in Figure A10.2 is in third normal form.

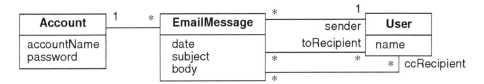

Figure A10.2 Revised email model in third normal form

10.3 Figure A10.3 shows the Hillard metrics for Exercise 3.6. The abbreviations at the top of the table correspond to the names on the left side of the table. Note that the metric is computed in terms of tables, so we must allow for the many-to-many association between *Make* and *Auto_Dealer*. Therefore, the geodesic distance from *Make* to *Physical_Vehicle* is 3 — *Make* to *Auto_Dealer__Make*, *Auto_Dealer__Make* to *Auto_Dealer*, and *Auto_Dealer* to *Physical_Vehicle*.

10.4 Figure A10.4 shows the Hillard metrics for the answer to Exercise 5.3. The abbreviations at the top of the table correspond to the names on the left side of the table. There are seven classes plus two many-to-many associations. The answer presumes that the superclass and subclasses are each implemented as a table. Therefore, the geodesic distance from *NutritionDescriptor* to *BaseIngredient* is 4 — *NutritionDescriptor* to *NutritionFact*, *NutritionFact* to *FoodProduct*, *FoodProduct* to *Ingredient*, and *Ingredient* to *BaseIngredient*

10.5 Figure A10.5 shows the Hillard metrics for Exercise 3.7. The abbreviations at the top of the table correspond to the names on the left side of the table. There are ten classes plus two many-to-many associations.

10.6 Figure A10.6 shows the Data Model Scorecard® for the online retail model using Hoberman's template. Of course, this is just a textbook example, so the weighting of categories and scores are subjective.

- Order: 6, Size: 6
- Average degree: 2.0 (*Make*–2, *Model*–2, *Trim*–2, *Physical_Vehicle*–2, *Auto_Dealer*–2, *Auto_Dealer__Make*–2)
- Average geodesic distance: 1.8, Maximum geodesic distance: 3

Geodesic distance

	Make	Model	Trim	PV	AD	AD_M
Make	XXX	1	2	3	2	1
Model	1	XXX	1	2	3	2
Trim	2	1	XXX	1	2	3
Physical_Vehicle	3	2	1	XXX	1	2
Auto_Dealer	2	3	2	1	XXX	1
Auto_Dealer__Make	1	2	3	2	1	XXX

Figure A10.3 Hillard complexity metrics for Exercise 3.6

- Order: 9, Size: 9
- Average degree: 2.0 (*NutritionDescriptor*–1, *NutritionFact*–2, *FoodProduct*–4, *FoodProduct__Allergen*–2, *Allergen*–1, *Ingredient*–4, *Ingredient__FoodProduct*–2, *BaseIngredient*–1, *Manufacturer*–1)
- Average geodesic distance: 2.4, Maximum geodesic distance: 4

Geodesic distance

	ND	NF	FP	FP_A	A	I	I_FP	BI	M
NutritionDescriptor	XX	1	2	3	4	3	3	4	4
NutritionFact	1	XX	1	2	3	2	2	3	3
FoodProduct	2	1	XX	1	2	1	1	2	2
FoodProduct__Allergen	3	2	1	XX	1	2	2	3	3
Allergen	4	3	2	1	XX	3	3	4	4
Ingredient	3	2	1	2	3	XX	1	1	1
Ingredient__FoodProduct	3	2	1	2	3	1	XX	2	2
BaseIngredient	4	3	2	3	4	1	2	XX	2
Manufacturer	4	3	2	3	4	1	2	2	XX

Figure A10.4 Hillard complexity metrics for the answer to Exercise 5.3

- Order: 12, Size: 15
- Average degree: 2.5 (*Institution*–3, *Department*–4, *Teacher*–3, *Department__Teacher*–2, *Student*–3, *ListedCourse*–2, *OfferedCourse*–6, *CourseRegistration*–2, *CourseTimeSlot*–1, *Textbook*–1, *OfferedCourse__Textbook*–2, *Location*–1)
- Average geodesic distance: 2.2, Maximum geodesic distance: 4

Geodesic distance

	I	D	T	D_T	S	LC	OC	CR	CTS	TB	OC_TB	L
Institution	X	1	1	2	1	2	2	2	3	4	3	3
Department	1	X	2	1	1	1	2	2	3	4	3	3
Teacher	1	2	X	1	2	2	1	2	2	3	2	2
Department__ Teacher	2	1	1	X	2	2	2	3	3	4	3	3
Student	1	1	2	2	X	3	2	1	3	4	3	3
ListedCourse	2	1	2	2	3	X	1	2	2	3	2	2
OfferedCourse	2	2	1	2	2	1	X	1	1	2	1	1
Course Registration	2	2	2	3	1	2	1	X	2	3	2	2
CourseTimeSlot	3	3	2	3	3	2	1	2	X	3	2	2
Textbook	4	4	3	4	4	3	2	3	3	X	1	3
OfferedCourse__ Textbook	3	3	2	3	3	2	1	2	2	1	X	2
Location	3	3	2	3	3	2	1	2	2	3	2	X

Figure A10.5 Hillard complexity metrics for Exercise 3.7

Data Model Scorecard® for the online retail model

#	Category	Total score	Model score	%	Comments
1	How well do the characteristics of the model support the type of model?	15	15	100	The model is an operational model that is fully normalized.
2	How well does the model capture the requirements?	15	15	100	The model captures the requirements as stated.
3	How complete is the model?	15	5	33	The model is clearly incomplete (as the requirements are incomplete), but suffices as an example.
4	How structurally sound is the model?	15	15	100	The model is sound.
5	How well does the model leverage generic structures?	10	10	100	The model seems fine in this regard.
6	How well does the model follow naming standards?	5	5	100	No naming standards were specified for this problem but the names seem clear.
7	How well has the model been arranged for readability?	5	5	100	There are no crossing lines and the model is compact.
8	How good are the definitions?	10	7	70	There are definitions but they could be elaborated.
9	How consistent is the model with the enterprise?	0	0	—	There is no enterprise model to compare against.
10	How well does the metadata match the data?	10	10	100	There are no misleading names.
	TOTAL SCORE	100	87		

Figure A10.6 Sample data model scorecard

Test 2

Congratulations if you get eight or more answers correct. Such a high score demonstrates that you understand the material well. If you score lower, you should go back and review the text and exercises.

Keep in mind that the test covers only some of the material in Part 2.

1. b   There is nothing in the model to prevent multiple persons from serving for an office.

For a wrong answer, see Section 7.1.

2. a   The first has existence-based identity and the second has value-based identity, but they describe the same UML models.

For a wrong answer, see Section 6.1 and Section 6.2.

3. a   Normally, a table should have a primary key, but it is not required. For example, a temporary table may not need a primary key.

For a wrong answer, see Section 6.1.

4. b   The right model violates third normal form. In the left model, *spCode* is unique, and therefore must have one *spName*. In the right model there is no enforced dependency of *spName* on *sp-Code*.

For a wrong answer, see Section 10.1.

5. b   With the model on the top, the same *Person* can be both a producer and writer, for example. For the model on the bottom, a *Person* can only assume a single role in making a movie. The bottom model has a many-to-many association between *Movie* and *Person*, and only a single *movieRole* can be assigned to the combination.

For a wrong answer, see Section 7.1.

6. b   You should explicitly model associations and not bury them as attributes.

For a wrong answer, see Chapters 4 and 7. Explicit, declarative relationship types are an emphasis of any kind of entity-relationship modeling (such as the UML). It is important that you understand this point.

7. a   See Section 4.4.

8. a   Note that the database for the model has two *Address* records that hold the same address data (one copy for Joe Brown and one copy for Sally Smith). The model has no constraint to prevent such duplicate address records from being stored. The model deliberately assigns *Address* to one *Customer*, is so that each *Address* record has clear ownership. If a *Customer* is deleted, then its *Addresses* can also be deleted. Otherwise, if *Addresses* were multiply referenced, there would be a risk of dangling references.

If you have a wrong answer and are confused (not just an accidental oversight), you need to revisit all of Parts 1 and 2. This is a basic question about the meaning of a model.

9. a   The top model is better. A *VendedProduct* is not a combination of an *OrderItem* and *Product* — that makes no sense. Furthermore, there can be multiple *VendedProducts* for a combination of an *OrderItem* and *Product* (such as different *VendedProducts* in various conditions).

For a wrong answer, see Section 7.1.

10. a   The subclasses have no data (attributes, associations) of their own, so there is no purpose to the generalization.

For a wrong answer, see Section 8.5.

Chapter 12

Some of the exercises have multiple correct answers.

12.1   Figure A12.1 shows the model for both customs forms. The model is generic so that we can accommodate the different data of each form.

The questions in the Canadian and American forms are arbitrary. There are additional questions that they could ask in the future. Also if we were to integrate a third country we might find further questions. For example, a customs form might ask about medical history.

Each *CustomsQuestion* is typed as being a general or a personal question. Some *CustomsQuestions* have *EnumeratedAnswers* and some do not. If there are *EnumeratedAnswers* then the *GeneralAnswer* must be one of the *EnumeratedAnswers*. Similar behavior applies to *PersonalAnswer*.

A *CustomsDeclaration* has multiple *GeneralAnswers*, one for each general *CustomsQuestion*. A *CustomsDeclaration* also has many *PersonalDeclarations*, one for each *Person* covered by the form (multiple family members). Each *PersonalDeclaration* consists of multiple *PersonalAnswers*, one for each personal *CustomsQuestion*.

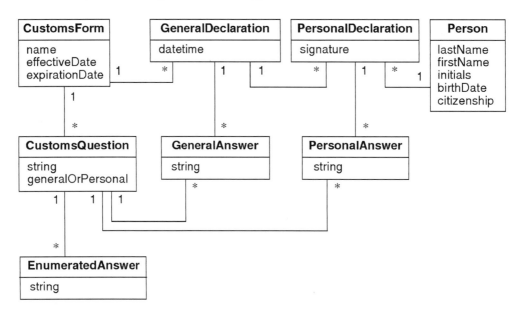

Figure A12.1 Model for Canadian and American customs data

12.2   Figure A12.2 shows an initial enterprise data model that includes major concepts from the auto insurance card model as well as the auto insurance bill model.

Figure A12.2 Initial EDM for auto insurance data

Chapter 13

Some of the exercises have multiple correct answers.

13.1   Figure A13.1 shows the data warehouse model for online auction data.

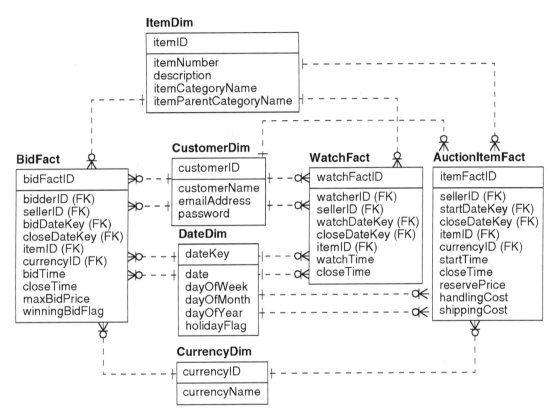

Figure A13.1 Data warehouse model for online auctions

- *Reply* and *Feedback* are not relevant for this exercise.
- *PaymentMethod* does not seem relevant to any of the facts.
- Note the two roles for *DateDim*. The facts refer to *DateDim* for the *bidDate*, *watchDate*, *startDate*, and *closeDate* so that the additional date convenience attributes are available (*dayOfWeek*, *dayOfMonth*, *dayOfYear*, and *holidayFlag*). The *bidTime*, *watchTime*, *startTime*, and *closeTime* attributes store the time for their corresponding dates.
- The bid and watch facts also have two roles for *Customer*.
- For *ItemDim*, we store the item category, as well as the immediate parent. Additional category attributes could be stored, if needed.

13.2   Figure A13.2 and Figure A13.3 show two options for snowflaking on *ItemDim*. As the text mentioned, you should forego snowflaking unless there is a very large dimension. For example, if the online auction application stored many more attributes for *Item* and *Customer*, they could be candidates for snowflaking.

13.3   Given that there is substantial subclass data, we would regard the third option as best; then it is possible to query across all transactions, as well as retrieve detail for the subclasses.

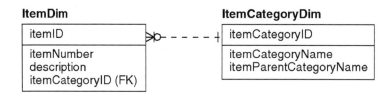

Figure A13.2 Snowflaking on *ItemDim*

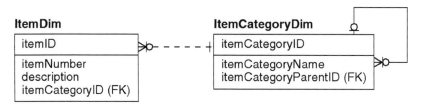

Figure A13.3 Snowflaking on *ItemDim*

13.4   Figure A13.4 shows Hillard metrics for Figure 13.1. The abbreviations at the top correspond to the names on the left side of the table.

- Order: 8, Size: 8
- Average degree: 2.0 (*OrderJunkDim*–1, *OrderFact*–3, *CustomerDim*–2, *DateDim*–2, *Product-Dim*–1, *VendedProductDim*-1, *OrderItemFact*–5, *MerchantDim*–1)
- Average geodesic distance: 2.1, Maximum geodesic distance: 4

Geodesic distance

	OF	OIF	OJD	CD	DD	PD	VPD	MD
OrderFact	XX	2	1	1	1	3	3	3
OrderItemFact	2	XX	3	1	1	1	1	1
OrderJunkDim	1	3	XX	2	2	4	4	4
CustomerDim	1	1	2	XX	2	2	2	2
DateDim	1	1	2	2	XX	2	2	2
ProductDim	3	1	4	2	2	XX	2	2
VendedProductDim	3	1	4	2	2	2	XX	2
MerchantDim	3	1	4	2	2	2	2	XX

Figure A13.4 Hillard complexity metrics for Figure 13.1

Chapter 14

Some of the exercises have multiple correct answers.

14.1 The model in Figure 8.10 is a suitable product master data model.

14.2 Figure A14.1 shows a master data model for census location. The *Location name* covers the *Country name*, *Region name*, *StateProvince name*, and so forth for all the subclasses. For reasons of layout, *CensusDesignatedPlace* is shown beneath the other subclasses, but all the subclasses are peers and of equal importance. The parent location is captured by the various associations on subclasses (*StreetAddress* to *City*, *City* to *County*, and so forth).

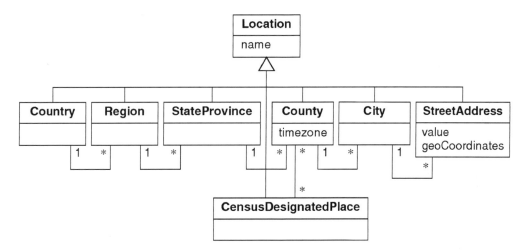

Figure A14.1 Master data model for census location

Test 3

Congratulations if you get four or more answers correct. Such a high score demonstrates that you understand the material well. If you score lower, you should go back and review the text and exercises. Keep in mind that the test covers only some of the material in Part 3.

1. c This is clearly a star schema. Facts are surrounded by multiple dimensions, some of which are conformed dimensions (shared). The facts have many multiplicity with respect to each dimension.

For a wrong answer, revisit Chapter 13 and pay attention to the explanation of a star schema.

2. b This is an enterprise data model. It is small in scope and focused on deep concepts that can underlie multiple applications.

For a wrong answer, reread Chapter 12.

3. a, c By definition an enterprise data model is supposed to be no more than a handful of tables. A master data model should not exceed a few dozen tables. Operational data models and data warehouses can have large numbers of tables.

For a wrong answer, revisit the chapters for the kinds of models that you have wrong.

4. b, c An enterprise data model is a guideline for an organization and need not have a physical model. Users cannot modify data warehouse data, so there are no user mistakes to guard against. ETL scripts periodically load application data, enforcing referential integrity as part of their data processing. Both operational data models and master data models concern data that users can update; referential integrity protects against user and application errors.

For a wrong answer, revisit the chapters for the kinds of models you have wrong.

5. a,b,c All three items are true. Conforming dimensions reduce the number of tables. More importantly, all queries are on the same basis, so that comparisons can be made. It is also important that the data warehouse be consistent, otherwise it is confusing to interpret the results of queries.

For a wrong answer revisit Chapter 13.

Chapter 15

15.1 Here is the database creation script for the answer to Exercise 7.9.

```
CREATE TABLE CourseRegistration (
    courseRegistrationID int identity(1,1) NOT NULL ,
    registrationDate      datetime  NULL ,
    terminationDate       datetime  NULL ,
    grade                 varchar(5)  NULL
      CHECK (grade IN ('A','B','C','D','F')),
    offeredCourseID       int NOT NULL ,
    studentID             int NOT NULL ,
CONSTRAINT pk_CR PRIMARY KEY (courseRegistrationID) );

CREATE INDEX i1_CR ON CourseRegistration ( offeredCourseID );

CREATE INDEX i2_CR ON CourseRegistration ( studentID );

CREATE TABLE CourseTimeSlot (
    courseTimeSlotID      int identity(1,1) NOT NULL ,
    endTime               datetime  NULL ,
    offeredCourseID       int NOT NULL ,
    dayOfWeek             varchar(20)  NOT NULL ,
    startTime             datetime  NOT NULL ,
CONSTRAINT pk_CTS PRIMARY KEY (courseTimeSlotID),
CONSTRAINT ak1_CTS
      UNIQUE (offeredCourseID, dayOfWeek, startTime) );

CREATE TABLE Department (
    departmentID          int identity(1,1) NOT NULL ,
    departmentName        varchar(50)  NOT NULL ,
    institutionID         int NOT NULL ,
    departmentCode        varchar(20)  NOT NULL ,
CONSTRAINT pk_dept PRIMARY KEY (departmentID),
CONSTRAINT ak1_dept UNIQUE (institutionID, departmentCode) );

CREATE TABLE Institution (
    institutionID         int identity(1,1) NOT NULL ,
    institutionName       varchar(50)  NOT NULL ,
CONSTRAINT pk_institution PRIMARY KEY (institutionID) );

CREATE TABLE IsMemberOf (
    departmentID          int NOT NULL ,
    teacherID             int NOT NULL ,
CONSTRAINT pk_ismemb PRIMARY KEY (departmentID, teacherID) );

CREATE INDEX i1_ismemb ON IsMemberOf ( teacherID );
```

Figure A15.1 Database creation script for the course model

```
CREATE TABLE ListedCourse (
    listedCourseID         int identity(1,1) NOT NULL ,
    courseName             varchar(50)  NOT NULL ,
    creditHours            int NULL ,
    description            varchar(254)  NULL ,
    departmentID           int NOT NULL ,
    year                   int NOT NULL ,
    courseCode             varchar(10)  NOT NULL ,
CONSTRAINT pk_LC PRIMARY KEY (listedCourseID),
CONSTRAINT ak1_LC UNIQUE (departmentID, year, courseCode) )

CREATE TABLE Location (
    locationID             int identity(1,1) NOT NULL ,
    locationName           varchar(50)  NOT NULL ,
CONSTRAINT pk_location PRIMARY KEY (locationID) );

CREATE TABLE OfferedCourse (
    offeredCourseID        int identity(1,1) NOT NULL ,
    startDate              datetime  NOT NULL ,
    duration               int NOT NULL ,
    listedCourseID         int NOT NULL ,
    semester               varchar(20)  NOT NULL ,
    sectionNumber          varchar(20)  NOT NULL ,
    locationID             int NOT NULL ,
    teacherID              int NOT NULL ,
CONSTRAINT pk_OC PRIMARY KEY (offeredCourseID),
CONSTRAINT ak1_OC
    UNIQUE (listedCourseID, semester, sectionNumber) );

CREATE INDEX i1_OC ON OfferedCourse ( locationID );

CREATE INDEX i2_OC ON OfferedCourse ( teacherID );

CREATE TABLE OfferedCourse_Textbook (
    offeredCourseID        int NOT NULL ,
    textbookID             int NOT NULL ,
CONSTRAINT pk_OCT PRIMARY KEY (offeredCourseID, textbookID) );

CREATE INDEX i1_OCT ON OfferedCourse_Textbook ( textbookID );

CREATE TABLE Student (
    studentID              int identity(1,1) NOT NULL ,
    studentName            varchar(50)  NOT NULL ,
    institutionID          int NOT NULL ,
    majorID                int NULL ,
CONSTRAINT pk_student PRIMARY KEY (studentID) );

CREATE INDEX i1_student ON Student ( institutionID );

CREATE INDEX i2_student ON Student ( majorID );
```

Figure A15.1 Database creation script for the course model (continued)

```
CREATE TABLE Teacher (
    teacherID              int identity(1,1) NOT NULL ,
    teacherName            varchar(50)  NOT NULL ,
    institutionID          int NOT NULL ,
CONSTRAINT pk_teacher PRIMARY KEY (teacherID) );

CREATE INDEX i1_teacher ON Teacher ( institutionID );

CREATE TABLE Textbook (
    textbookID             int identity(1,1) NOT NULL ,
    textbookName           varchar(50)  NOT NULL ,
CONSTRAINT pk_textbook PRIMARY KEY (textbookID) );

ALTER TABLE CourseRegistration ADD CONSTRAINT fk1_CR
FOREIGN KEY (offeredCourseID) REFERENCES OfferedCourse
ON DELETE NO ACTION;

ALTER TABLE CourseRegistration ADD CONSTRAINT fk2_CR
FOREIGN KEY (studentID) REFERENCES Student
ON DELETE NO ACTION;

ALTER TABLE CourseTimeSlot ADD CONSTRAINT fk1_CTS
FOREIGN KEY (offeredCourseID) REFERENCES OfferedCourse
ON DELETE NO ACTION;

ALTER TABLE Department ADD CONSTRAINT fk1_dept
FOREIGN KEY (institutionID) REFERENCES Institution
ON DELETE NO ACTION;

ALTER TABLE IsMemberOf ADD CONSTRAINT fk1_ismemb
FOREIGN KEY (departmentID) REFERENCES Department
ON DELETE NO ACTION;

ALTER TABLE IsMemberOf ADD CONSTRAINT fk2_ismemb
FOREIGN KEY (teacherID) REFERENCES Teacher
ON DELETE NO ACTION;

ALTER TABLE ListedCourse ADD CONSTRAINT fk1_LC
FOREIGN KEY (departmentID) REFERENCES Department
ON DELETE NO ACTION;

ALTER TABLE OfferedCourse ADD CONSTRAINT fk1_OC
FOREIGN KEY (listedCourseID) REFERENCES ListedCourse
ON DELETE NO ACTION;

ALTER TABLE OfferedCourse ADD CONSTRAINT fk2_OC
FOREIGN KEY (locationID) REFERENCES Location
ON DELETE NO ACTION;

ALTER TABLE OfferedCourse ADD CONSTRAINT fk3_OC
FOREIGN KEY (teacherID) REFERENCES Teacher
ON DELETE NO ACTION;
```

Figure A15.1 Database creation script for the course model (continued)

```
ALTER TABLE OfferedCourse_Textbook ADD CONSTRAINT fk1_OCT
FOREIGN KEY (offeredCourseID) REFERENCES OfferedCourse
ON DELETE NO ACTION;

ALTER TABLE OfferedCourse_Textbook ADD CONSTRAINT fk2_OCT
FOREIGN KEY (textbookID) REFERENCES Textbook
ON DELETE NO ACTION;

ALTER TABLE Student ADD CONSTRAINT fk1_student
FOREIGN KEY (institutionID) REFERENCES Institution
ON DELETE NO ACTION;

ALTER TABLE Student ADD CONSTRAINT fk2_student
FOREIGN KEY (majorID) REFERENCES Department
ON DELETE NO ACTION;

ALTER TABLE Teacher ADD CONSTRAINT fk1_teacher
FOREIGN KEY (institutionID) REFERENCES Institution
ON DELETE NO ACTION;
```

Figure A15.1 Database creation script for the course model (continued)

15.2   Here is the database creation script for the answer to Exercise 5.3.

```
CREATE TABLE Allergen (
    allergenID              int identity(1,1) NOT NULL ,
    allergenName            varchar(50)  NOT NULL ,
CONSTRAINT pk_allergen PRIMARY KEY (allergenID),
CONSTRAINT ak1_allergen UNIQUE (allergenName) );

CREATE TABLE BaseIngredient (
    baseIngredientID     int NOT NULL ,
CONSTRAINT pk_BI PRIMARY KEY (baseIngredientID) );

CREATE TABLE FoodProduct (
    foodProductID           int NOT NULL ,
    foodProductCode         varchar(20)  NOT NULL ,
    servingSize             varchar(50)  NULL ,
CONSTRAINT pk_FP PRIMARY KEY (foodProductID) );

CREATE TABLE FoodProduct_Allergen (
    foodProductID           int NOT NULL ,
    allergenID              int NOT NULL ,
CONSTRAINT pk_FPA PRIMARY KEY (foodProductID, allergenID) );

CREATE INDEX i1_FPA ON FoodProduct_Allergen ( allergenID );
```

Figure A15.2 Database creation script for the food product model

```
CREATE TABLE FoodProduct_Ingredient (
    foodProductID          int NOT NULL ,
    ingredientID           int NOT NULL ,
CONSTRAINT pk_FPI PRIMARY KEY (foodProductID, ingredientID) );

CREATE INDEX i1_FPI ON FoodProduct_Ingredient ( ingredientID );

CREATE TABLE Ingredient (
    ingredientID           int identity(1,1) NOT NULL ,
    ingredientName         varchar(50)  NOT NULL ,
    ingredientDiscrim      varchar(20)  NOT NULL
        CHECK  (ingredientDiscrim IN
        ('FoodProduct', 'BaseIngredient')),
    manufacturerID         int NOT NULL ,
CONSTRAINT pk_ingred PRIMARY KEY (ingredientID),
CONSTRAINT ak1_ingred UNIQUE (ingredientName) );

CREATE INDEX i1_ingred ON Ingredient ( manufacturerID );

CREATE TABLE Manufacturer (
    manufacturerID         int identity(1,1) NOT NULL ,
    manufacturerName       varchar(50)  NOT NULL ,
    address                varchar(254)  NULL ,
    phoneNumber            varchar(20)  NULL ,
    website                varchar(50)  NULL ,
CONSTRAINT pk_manuf PRIMARY KEY (manufacturerID ) );

CREATE TABLE NutritionDescriptor (
    nutritionDescriptorID int identity(1,1) NOT NULL ,
    nutritionDescriptorName varchar(50)  NOT NULL ,
CONSTRAINT pk_ND PRIMARY KEY (nutritionDescriptorID),
CONSTRAINT ak1_ND UNIQUE (nutritionDescriptorName) );

CREATE TABLE NutritionFact (
    nutritionFactID        int identity(1,1) NOT NULL ,
    servingAmount          varchar(50)  NULL ,
    dailyValuePercent      numeric(3)  NULL ,
    foodProductID          int NOT NULL ,
    nutritionDescriptorID int NOT NULL ,
CONSTRAINT pk_NF PRIMARY KEY (foodProductID ) );

CREATE INDEX i1_NF ON NutritionFact ( foodProductID );

CREATE INDEX i2_NF ON NutritionFact ( nutritionDescriptorID );

ALTER TABLE BaseIngredient ADD CONSTRAINT fk1_BI
FOREIGN KEY (baseIngredientID) REFERENCES Ingredient
ON DELETE CASCADE;

ALTER TABLE FoodProduct ADD CONSTRAINT fk1_FP
FOREIGN KEY (foodProductID) REFERENCES Ingredient
ON DELETE CASCADE;
```

Figure A15.2 Database creation script for the food product model (continued)

```
ALTER TABLE FoodProduct_Allergen ADD CONSTRAINT fk1_FPA
FOREIGN KEY (foodProductID) REFERENCES FoodProduct
ON DELETE NO ACTION;

ALTER TABLE FoodProduct_Allergen ADD CONSTRAINT fk2_FPA
FOREIGN KEY (allergenID) REFERENCES Allergen
ON DELETE NO ACTION;

ALTER TABLE FoodProduct_Ingredient ADD CONSTRAINT fk1_FPI
FOREIGN KEY (foodProductID) REFERENCES FoodProduct
ON DELETE NO ACTION;

ALTER TABLE FoodProduct_Ingredient ADD CONSTRAINT fk2_FPI
FOREIGN KEY (ingredientID) REFERENCES Ingredient
ON DELETE NO ACTION;

ALTER TABLE Ingredient ADD CONSTRAINT fk1_ingred
FOREIGN KEY (manufacturerID) REFERENCES Manufacturer
ON DELETE NO ACTION;

ALTER TABLE NutritionFact ADD CONSTRAINT fk1_NF
FOREIGN KEY (foodProductID) REFERENCES FoodProduct
ON DELETE NO ACTION;

ALTER TABLE NutritionFact ADD CONSTRAINT fk2_NF
FOREIGN KEY (nutritionDescriptorID) REFERENCES NutritionDescriptor
ON DELETE NO ACTION;
```

Figure A15.2 Database creation script for the food product model (continued)

Chapter 16

16.1 Here is the database traversal expression for the OCL expression.
aProduct.VendedProduct.Review.Review_Rating.rater->asSet().
Here is SQL code.
SELECT DISTINCT customerID
FROM Product P
INNER JOIN VendedProduct VP ON P.productID = VP.productID
INNER JOIN Review R ON VP.vendedProductID = R.vendedProductID
INNER JOIN Review_Rating RR ON R.reviewID = RR.reviewID
INNER JOIN Customer C ON RR.raterID = C.customerID;

16.2

   a. Here are the answers for the first query.

   - **Business intent**
     For what course names is a student registered in a specified semester?

   - **OCL expression**
     aStudent.CourseRegistration.OfferedCourse->select(semester = aSemester).ListedCourse. courseName

   - **Table traversal**
     aStudent.CourseRegistration.OfferedCourse->select(semester = aSemester).ListedCourse. courseName

   - **SQL code**
     SELECT S.studentID, S.studentName, LC.courseName
     FROM Student S
     INNER JOIN CourseRegistration CR ON S.studentID = CR.studentID
     INNER JOIN OfferedCourse OC ON CR.offeredCourseID = OC.offeredCourseID
     INNER JOIN ListedCourse LC ON OC.listedCourseID = LC.listedCourseID
     WHERE OC.semester = aSemester;   -- aSemester is a parameter

   b. Here are the answers for the second query. The major department for a student is optional, but only students with a major are relevant. (Therefore the query has an inner join and not an outer join.) The *self* refers to a *CourseRegistration*.

   - **Business intent**
     What is the average grade for a student in courses for their major department?

   - **OCL expression**
     aStudent.CourseRegistration->select(self IN major.ListedCourse.OfferedCourse. CourseRegistration).grade->average()

   - **Table traversal**
     aStudent.CourseRegistration->select(self IN major.ListedCourse.OfferedCourse. CourseRegistration).grade->average()

   - **SQL code**
     SELECT S.studentID, S.studentName,
        avg (CASE CR.grade
           WHEN 'A' THEN 4
           WHEN 'B' THEN 3
           WHEN 'C' THEN 2
           WHEN 'D' THEN 1
           ELSE 0
        END) AS averageGrade
     FROM Student S

INNER JOIN CourseRegistration CR ON S.studentID = CR.studentID
WHERE CR.courseRegistrationID IN (
  SELECT CR2.courseRegistrationID
  FROM Student S2
  INNER JOIN Department D ON S2.majorID = D.departmentID
  INNER JOIN ListedCourse LC ON D.departmentID = LC.departmentID
  INNER JOIN OfferedCourse OC ON LC.listedCourseID = OC.listedCourseID
  INNER JOIN CourseRegistration CR2 ON OC.offeredCourseID = CR2.offeredCourseID)
GROUP BY S.studentID, S.studentName;

16.3 This exercise illustrates the need for an outer join.

- **Business intent**
  Return data for the Transactions for a CheckingAccount including data about the Statement, if the Transaction has been listed on one.

- **OCL expression**
  aCheckingAccount.Transaction + aCheckingAccount.Transaction.Statement

- **Table traversal**
  aCheckingAccount.Transaction + aCheckingAccount.Transaction.Statement

- **SQL code**
  SELECT T.transactionID, T.referenceNumber, T.postingDate, T.transactionAmount,
    T.description, S.statementID, S.statementBeginDate, S.statementEndDate,
    S.statementBeginBalance, S.statementEndBalance
  FROM CheckingAccount CA
  INNER JOIN Transaction T ON CA.checkingAccountID = T.checkingAccountID
  LEFT OUTER JOIN Statement S ON T.statementID = S.statementID
  WHERE CA.checkingAccountID = aCheckingAccount;
    -- aCheckingAccount is a parameter

Test 4

Congratulations if you get four or more answers correct. Such a high score demonstrates that you understand the material well. If you score lower, you should go back and review the text and exercises.

Keep in mind that the test covers only some of the material in Part 4.

1. b   It is clearly better to first specify domains and use the domains to determine the appropriate data type for each attribute. Some database design tools facilitate this indirection, but regardless, there is no reason you cannot think in terms of domains. Section 3.4 explains further about the benefits of using domains.

For a wrong answer, reread Section 15.2.

2. c   Database managers generate an index as a side effect of each primary and alternate key constraint. Therefore, there is no point to your creating a redundant index in addition to that which is already implicitly created.

For a wrong answer, reread Section 15.4.

3. b   As much as possible, it is important to assure the quality of the data in a database. The referential integrity mechanism built into relational databases is highly efficient and guarantees that there are no dangling references to data. (Data warehouses are an exception to this rule.)

For a wrong answer, reread Section 15.5.

4. b   Traversal to an association end with zero or one multiplicity can result in an outer join, but need not. For example, a SQL query for the answer to Exercise 7.10 would not result in an outer join if we were only considering *Transactions* that were listed in some *Statement*.

For a wrong answer, reread Section 16.6.

5. d   All these items are reasons why a data model is more than a specification of structure, but also covers important aspects of business computations.

For a wrong answer, reread Section 16.2.

Index

Made in the USA
San Bernardino, CA
09 March 2016